FROM COMMUNISM TO CAPITALISM

ALSO AVAILABLE FROM BLOOMSBURY

Barbarism, Michel Henry
Seeing the Invisible, Michel Henry

FROM COMMUNISM TO CAPITALISM

Theory of a Catastrophe

Michel Henry
Translated by
Scott Davidson

BLOOMSBURY
LONDON • NEW DELHI • NEW YORK • SYDNEY

Bloomsbury Academic

An imprint of Bloomsbury Publishing Plc

50 Bedford Square	1385 Broadway
London	New York
WC1B 3DP	NY 10018
UK	USA

www.bloomsbury.com

Bloomsbury is a registered trade mark of Bloomsbury Publishing Plc

This book is the English edition of "*Du Communisme au Capitalisme. Théorie d'une catastrophe*" © Université Catholique de Louvain

This English translation © Bloomsbury Publishing Plc, 2014

British Library Cataloguing-in-Publication Data
A catalogue record for this book is available from the British Library.

ISBN: HB: 978-1-4725-2431-7
ePDF: 978-1-4725-3183-4
ePub: 978-1-4725-2608-3

Library of Congress Cataloging-in-Publication Data
A catalog record for this book is available from the Library of Congress.

Typeset by Fakenham Prepress Solutions, Fakenham Norfolk NR21 8NN
Printed and bound in India

CONTENTS

TRANSLATOR'S PREFACE

SCOTT DAVIDSON

Michel Henry's book *From Communism to Capitalism: Theory of a Catastrophe* was originally published in 1991. The book was written ostensibly in response to the sudden and catastrophic collapse of the Eastern bloc in the late 1980s. Westerners watched in fascination as unprecedented masses of people gathered in the public squares of Eastern capitals. Of course, this was not the first time that they had called for economic and political reform. What was unprecedented, however, was the fact that their calls were not censored or met with state violence. Instead, the masses of protestors were joined in the streets by the very same government and military officials who had oppressed them before but who now echoed their demands for reform. What is the underlying cause behind this turn of events? To answer this question, *From Communism to Capitalism* applies the conceptual tools established in Henry's philosophy of life to unveil the deep significance underlying the abrupt transformation of the Eastern bloc at the time.

The great value of Henry's book for readers today, in my opinion, does not reside so much in what Henry had to say about the events that took place in the East but in his prognosis of what this transition "from communism to capitalism" would bring about in our time. Communism and capitalism, according to Henry, are two faces of the same death. For it turns out that they are plagued by the same crisis: a crisis of the individual. This leads Henry to suspect that the economic and political reforms in the Eastern bloc may be unable to deliver the liberation and prosperity that they promise. Instead, it is likely that they will become yet another iteration of the attack on the individual.

Henry's suspicions, it could be argued, were realized in the Global Financial Crisis of 2008, if not before. This time, the sudden and dramatic collapse did not befall communist countries, instead its effects rippled across the global system of capitalism. People across the world witnessed the simultaneous collapse of the world's largest banks, the rapid growth of paralyzing national debt, sharp declines in the value of financial markets, and real estate value, along with sharp increases in rates of unemployment. To mitigate these problems, massive financial bailouts of industries, banks and entire governments were implemented. These bailouts were subsidized primarily by individual taxpayers—the very same ones who had suffered from the effects of the economic collapse itself—although these very same individuals were mostly left to suffer the effects of this crisis on their own. Years later, cautious reports of a gradual recovery from this economic downturn are beginning to emerge, however these very same reports are often couched in an air of uncertainty. They leave open the threat of a second and perhaps irrecoverable collapse to follow.

Various explanations of the cause of this global economic crisis have been offered: greed in the real estate sector, risky behavior in the banking sector, and regulatory failures in the government sector. But, do such explanations truly go deep enough to capture this collapse in its full, global magnitude? They offer what might be called an internal critique of capitalism, inasmuch as they identify specific problems within specific sectors of the economy, say, with certain lending practices in banks or with failures of government oversight. As such, they propose to address those specific flaws through particular policy reforms in various sectors of the economy. But, if those analyses could be said to fall short, it would be for their inability to conceptualize this failure on a broader, systemic level. And, indeed, the great benefit of Henry's book for readers today is that it fills this critical gap by providing a cogent external critique of global capitalism.

Before elaborating the key elements of this critique, however, it is first necessary to situate *From Communism to Capitalism* within the broader context of Henry's oeuvre. Michel Henry (1922–2002) was a leading French philosopher and author whose writings spanned the latter half of the twentieth century. His primary emphasis throughout was on the development of his own philosophy of life. In his view, Western philosophy traditionally has been a philosophy of representation, or in other words, a philosophy of the relation between ideas in the mind and objects in the world. Due to its representational aim, it thereby ends up missing the essential meaning of life. If life is considered at all, it is understood primarily in biological terms, either as a property of objects in the world or as a process that takes place within a body. For Henry, however, the essential significance of life is not biological, instead it must be traced back to subjective lived experience. Life, as his work tirelessly points out, is neither an object of representation, nor a physical process; instead, it is fundamentally an affective experience in which one experiences one's own living. In this auto-affective experience, one has an immediate and non-differentiated relation to oneself that is distinct from any other type of relation that the self enters into with the world or others. This discovery of the auto-affective experience of one's own life provides a new starting point through which Henry sets out to re-map and re-envision the trajectory of philosophy. Clearly, this unique philosophy of life clearly informs and guides much of Henry's analysis, but it should also be noted that *From Communism to Capitalism* has an especially strong connection to two of his earlier works: *Marx* (1975) and *Barbarism* (1987).[1]

Henry's critique of communism in the first four chapters of the book borrows heavily from his earlier two-volume work on *Marx*, and readers will likely welcome his ability to condense the lengthy argument developed there. Henry's study of Marx set out to distinguish Marx's philosophy from Marxism, which he defined as the "interrelated set of misinterpretations that have been given concerning Marx." That is to say that the fundamental concepts of Marxism—productive forces, social classes, History, etc.—are not at all the fundamental concepts of Marx's own thought. In fact, they stand Marx's thought on its head, because these abstractions don't have explanatory value but rather need to be explained. Instead, Henry shows that Marx seeks to explicate their meaning through a return to their subjective origin, that is, to the living praxis of the individual.

The living individual is the non-economic origin of every society and economy. But, the fault of Marxism is not that it simply ignores the living individual but that it actively turns against it. This occurs, for instance, by granting priority to the abstract notion of "social class" over the living individual. If Society, History, or Class are taken as ultimate realities, then the individual would seem to be extraneous to them. This becomes the basis for the Marxist attack on the individual. It ends up eliminating or purging the living individuals who are its true foundation and who are the source of all economic value. By failing to appreciate this original source of value, Marxism placed the so-called "communist" countries on the wrong footing from the outset, and, as a result, rendered their eventual collapse inevitable.

While the analysis in the early chapters of *From Communism to Capitalism* borrows heavily from Henry's earlier writings on Marx, the later chapters of the book have a close connection to its immediate predecessor, *Barbarism*. Originally published in 1987, *Barbarism* was the only one of Henry's books ever to make it onto the French best-seller list. This was due primarily to the controversy sparked by its thesis. Henry contends that barbarism is not the result of individual or group psychology, neither is it tied to primitive forms of culture. Quite the contrary, even though Western thought has long been associated precisely with civilization and progress, Henry identifies it with the essence of barbarism. This claim is supported primarily through a careful analysis of the rise of the Galilean science.

Galileo's point of departure is to set aside everything that is merely subjective and to focus exclusively on what is observable, measurable, and quantifiable—in short, on what is "objective." What Henry criticizes here is not Galilean science as such, but the ideology that accompanies it: the scientific worldview. This ideology extends the Galilean approach beyond the realm of the natural sciences and seeks to apply it to all phenomena whatsoever. In other words, it maintains that the scientific method is the only legitimate way of knowing, and it condemns, in turn, all other ways of knowing: history, literature, art, and so forth. But, on Henry's view, all of these cultural forms are the products of life. So, to set them aside and invalidate them is ultimately to turn against life. This is why Henry comes to regard the encroachment of the scientific worldview and of technology onto all aspects of life as the true face of barbarism today.

Not surprisingly, Henry's book was the topic of heated discussion at the time of its publication, especially with regard to its harsh criticisms of technology, the media, and university reforms at the time. It evoked strong criticisms from reviewers. One line of criticism contended that Henry's claims about science and technology were one-sided and ignored many of the positive contributions that have been gained through the course of their development. Other reviewers were more sympathetic to Henry's views but yet raised the question of whether Henry really needed the elaborate theoretical and conceptual edifice of the book in order to arrive at conclusions that are more or less banal: that technology permeates all aspects of life today, that the media are taking the place of traditional forms of culture, and that universities are now guided by other pursuits than that of knowledge, such as profit or job training. It is especially worthwhile to address this latter point, as it is likely to be a sentiment felt not only by readers of *Barbarism* but by those of *From Communism to Capitalism* as well.

It should be noted that in both cases Henry is doing something quite different from ordinary news reporting, which simply sets out to describe or to comment on current events. Such accounts, on Henry's view, remain merely superficial, because they only grasp the actuality of events but fail to appreciate current events as historical products that need to be under-stood historically. The task of the intellectual historian, accordingly, is to reveal the meaning of current events by reconstructing the chain of events, concepts, and theories that have paved the way for them. This attempt to understand events within their intellectual lineage accounts not only for the elaborate constructions in his book but also for their critical depth.

In addition to the similarity between their methodological approaches, *From Communism to Capitalism* and *Barbarism* are also connected through their assessment that technology is a negation of life. *From Communism to Capitalism* adds an economic layer to this analysis. Technology comes into play with respect to one of the contradictions of capitalism. On the one hand, capitalism recognizes the productive value of the individual and transforms human history through its embrace of individual labor power. But, on the other hand, the aim of capitalism is the production of surplus value. Here individual labor becomes subsumed under the overarching goal of producing an abstraction: profit. Since capitalism is always in search of increased profits, this leads to increased pressure to exploit labor power more and more.

But there are limits on how much value an individual worker can produce. And it is in order to satisfy the perpetual demands to increase profits that another factor enters into the process of production and transforms it: technology. Technology progressively enhances the speed of production and decreases the need for individual workers. It transforms the process of production into an automated or mechanical process that is designed solely for the sake of producing profit. As a result, technology unhinges capitalism's connection to the living individual and abandons the productive force of the individual. By giving rise to unemployment, impoverishment, and idleness, this form of techno-capitalism rejoins Marxism as an attack on the individual.

It was out of the misery and despair that were suffered in the Eastern bloc countries that massive protests and economic reforms were introduced in the late 1980s and early 1990s. They looked to Western liberal democracies and capitalist economies for liberation from their condition. But can they really expect to find salvation through this "liberation" movement? Henry's answer is not optimistic. He predicts that the journey of the Eastern bloc countries toward a "free" market economy is likely to be analogous to the fabled "rendezvous at Samarkand." They will flee the death and despair that surrounds them only in order to find themselves under attack yet again. This is because—from communism to capitalism—we encounter the same result: two faces of the same death.

***

Let me add a few brief notes on the translation of this book. As I've noted in previous translations, Henry's style does not lend itself easily to the stylistic conventions of written English. To make the book more palatable for English readers, I have frequently modified his style by breaking down his elaborately constructed sentences into simpler, more direct ones. In so doing, I always have sought to leave the argument unaltered. I have also retained all italics from the original text, since Henry often uses them to emphasize key points.

One troublesome expression in the work is the French "*force de travail*." Here, as with the other Marxian terminology, I have employed the equivalent in Marx, which is "labor power." It bears noting, however, that this obscures the connection to the concept of force, a concept which appears frequently in Henry's other writings, for instance in his description of life as a force. I mention this point here so that readers are aware of this implicit connection that gets lost in translation.

INTRODUCTION: THE FAILURE OF SOCIALISM

Today one observes everywhere, at least throughout Europe, the collapse of the so-called socialist regimes. What is most striking about this upheaval, which is spreading out like a tidal wave sweeping up everything it passes over, is that it is occurring simultaneously in different places, thus overcoming national differences and historical particularities. From this it derives a characteristic that is both irresistible and universal: that of a revolution. As an event that comes from the root of things and remains indifferent to superficial phenomena, it calls for an explanation on the same scale. Neither empirical circumstances nor happenstance conditions that vary from one place to another can explain this powerful convergence. It requires a principle, a meta-historical reason, which one might be tempted to call metaphysical. Its failure should be made intelligible through a weakness or vice that is intrinsic to socialism, inasmuch as it is happening everywhere in an inexorable way.

One might be tempted, to be sure, to interpret this strange convergence of revolutionary movements in Warsaw, Leipzig, Budapest, Prague, and Bucharest, which have not even spared the Soviet Union itself in the form of nationalist protests, through considerations that are less ambitious and narrower. The simultaneous opening of spaces of contestation is coupled with a meaningful analogy. This concerns the unfolding of the process of revolutionary protest with, on the one hand, large popular gatherings, and, on the other hand, an unprecedented self-criticism of the ruling communist parties which abruptly decided to transform themselves entirely, even to suppress themselves purely and simply in order to make room for more "democratic" formations.

Communism, one could say, is carried away by a groundswell and is no longer up to the task of controlling a popular movement of this scale. It has no other solution than to join it in order to recapture it, or at least to go along with it for the moment and travel in the direction of the prevailing winds. Such an explanation raises doubts, however. Beyond a mere desire for protest or reform, the staunch desire to get rid of a hated regime, the hatred toward its leaders, its institutions, and its multiple problems is something that has existed from the outset in all of the countries that have been subjected to communism. It just happens to be the case that this deep dissatisfaction did not have an opportunity to manifest itself, because its slightest expression meant prison or death for those who would have had the imprudence to give in to it. The crowds could only enter the squares to claim their desire for liberation and change because tanks did not appear across from them or on other streets. With a few machine guns one can hold onto a town. Crowds and armies can only stand side by side when, tacitly or not, an agreement has already been sealed somewhere.

The question is thus: this time, why did the army receive the order to stay in its quarters or to go into the crowd only to fraternize with it? Why was this crowd authorized, even invited, to publicly express an opposition that in other times each individual had to keep bottled up and could not even risk a single look that might betray it? Why in the end did this dogmatic and stone-faced party —which was retaliatory, terrible, always correct, and continually rewriting history to fit the lies of the present—waver? Why did those in charge of the most unyielding dictatorships suddenly run to join the cohort of those whom they had oppressed for half a century? Why did the men of the party apparatus themselves—the worst conservatives, the heaviest bureaucrats, and the beneficiaries of titles—sound the call for a major reform?

Here it is hardly possible to avoid the hypothesis that there was a Plan. In fact, communism knows something about plans. Its specialty, its daily bread, is making a series of plans, five-year plans and assorted other ones, even though it should be noted that this activity itself does not make bread or any other consumable good but only misery and hunger. But when shortages become unbearable and call into question the very existence of society and its sheer survival, the final plan that comes to mind is the call for help. This is the only possible recourse for a regime that has destroyed all desire for work, all courage and confidence in the individuals that it has subjugated, and knows that it can no longer count on itself. In spite of all the external and internal decoys it has used, it has become aware of its own failure, and it has no other solution than to turn toward a more wealthy and sympathetic neighbor in the hope of salvation. This salvation includes everything that is lacking: supplies, all kinds of consumer goods, equipment, capital, investment, technology, and even, if possible, the trappings of culture for those who have destroyed every form of culture.

All of the know-how that is needed for daily life has simply ceased to be possible. The great change of direction of Soviet politics happened at this moment: when, by setting aside a blind ideology, those who were able to understand and held a remnant of power in a country given over to anarchy, to the pillage of public goods and to widescale corruption—when they judged that it was time to turn toward the West to ask not only for urgent aid but also for the formulas, the modes of management and production, that a society needs today in order to avoid ruin.

They are the leaders of the KGB, the only healthy and organized body in the nation that are not preoccupied with daily violations but with service to the State—the Soviet State that was falling apart. Let's follow Alain Besançon's analysis for a moment.[1] Under the impulse of its head Andropov, who then became head of the USSR, the KGB opens various Institutes of study whose aim is to acquire a precise knowledge of all sorts of methodologies in use in Western countries that ensure their success (or what seemed to be their success when seen from Moscow). In spite of its systematic character, this economic, technological, and even ideological espionage is no longer sufficient. It is also necessary to be able to use the knowledge discovered. A minimal level of organization must remain in the production apparatus in order to be able to integrate it. This is no longer the case when both products and the tools of production are the targets of daily theft by those who come into contact with them. Trucks, tractors, and cars disappear, piece by piece, on their delivery trips. That is frustrating. But when the parts that are needed in order to make them disappear from the factory, that is what definitively paralyzes any economy. Internal corruption had reached such a scale that the external aid to remedy had to be complete. It would be necessary to provide not only the missing products and necessary technologies but also the buildings, engineers, workforce, and even the police whose task was to prevent pillage. It would be necessary to change, as is said, not only the regime but the people.

This massive economic, scientific, and technical aid comes with a political condition, however. Appealing to Western democracies in order to obtain what they urgently need, the Soviet leaders are required to speak a language that is new to them, the language of democracy. In all the communist regions and countries, it is thereby important for deep "changes" to occur, political changes whose aim is to hide the economic failure as well as to seduce the West. Television viewers in the West thus watched a powerful drama with great delight: the abrupt and unforeseen return of the truth to the very same places where it had perished.

The first appearance or re-appearance of democracy were these large gatherings where the "people" itself appeared and showed its face—it had never had a face and no one had ever seen it before. These enormous, colossal gatherings whose numbers grew in a breathtaking fashion, like the sales figures of best-sellers, were offered by the media every day, evening, and night. At some point, one might come to believe that it was only there where it was crushed that freedom truly existed and that, as for lessons about democracy, nowadays they came to us from the East.

The first political demand of democracy is pluralism: no more single party rule! And from whom does one see this demand for the suppression of single party rule being made with an impressive cast every day, evening, and night? From the single party itself. Under various new banners loudly demanding the return of freedom and claiming their belief in its power, one should expect to see the sinister faces of those who trampled over it for decades. These reformers have followed along and made their careers in the shadows of the historical leaders who were suddenly turned out. As for the elimination of these leaders—whether it takes the form of a polite and simple retirement, a summary execution, or a spectacular trial—one tends to forget that this is a fixed rule of these regimes. The liquidation of those who have been compromised by obeying orders and thus can no longer survive, and are replaced by a clean, new layer—whose own turpitude is not yet known—this is a Stalinist purge.

Whatever masks this purge might hide behind whatever powers might have chosen it—whether it was the KGB or not—a set of facts is now evident to us: The great "democratic" uprising was chosen by the party itself. This does not imply that the public gatherings that occurred one after another in the Fall of 1989 in various capitals in the East did not correspond with the deep dissatisfaction of the population. In most of these countries, this dissatisfaction goes all the way back to the establishment of the communist regimes. These regimes, one should not forget, were imposed on entire peoples through a type of political violence that is constitutive of fascism. Can one risk to say and write it today in our so-called "free" countries? Popular democracies were not only dictatorial regimes—the communist party's self-proclaimed "dictatorship of the proletariat" works and fights in the name of the former—they were also the fascist regimes whose principles we will study later. Here we are limited to observing that fascism resides in a usurpation of the individual will and in physical coercion. Even in the USSR, dissatisfaction continued to grow—in spite of the gradual wearing down of the population by indoctrination, poverty, and alcoholism—to the point that the regime had, so to speak, proved its worth.

But this widespread dissatisfaction would not have been able to manifest itself, at least in the satellite countries, if the rulers had not chosen it somehow. Here the political maneuver adeptly performed and orchestrated by the media must be regarded as an extraordinary success. Where in the world do crowds assemble to display their desire for liberation and where is the democratic ideal alive, visible, and functioning? And under the aegis of who? Of the party that had put into place the most terrible regime and had constructed the most astounding synthesis of dictatorship and fascism that had ever been seen. It now appears as the great innovative force of the era, and its leader becomes an object of admiration by the whole world!

The democratic masquerade of the party does not happen without serious inconveniences. It shakes up the totalitarian regime that it had put into place, both from the outside by risking the loss of its colonies as well as from within where the call for liberty awakens nationalities and threatens to explode an ill-assorted empire. It is thus under the harshest necessity that it resorted to pursue the stopgap of freedom. What necessity is that? Here an undeniable fact emerges before us: today the economic failure of the socialist camp constrains it, and, in order to save itself, it is forced to play the card of opening to the West and to democracy. This gives rise to the true question, the one which motivated this work and to which it will try to respond: *What is the cause of the economic failure of socialism?*

A question like this has multiple aspects. In the first place, its scope is universal in the sense that, *on the economic level, communism failed everywhere that it was applied.* This failure affects the lives of millions of men and women. They surely did not rise up in order to drop a vote in the ballot box every four or five years, to elect a more or less paranoid president and to form a new list out of deputies who are thirsty for power and privilege. Nor did they do this for a "freedom of thought" that will become what it already is in "democracies"—the freedom of the media to brutalize and subjugate them. These men and women rose up in order to live and to have the right to live, to put an end to their suffering and misery. And the West is really only, in their eyes, as equivocal as this representation may sound, the image of what they do not have: an immediate happiness. In the streets of Budapest, freedom has already received its true name and is leading Hungary toward its future culture: McDonald's.

We should note in passing that to recognize the universality of the economic failure of communism is necessarily to denounce a certain number of lies that have accompanied communism since its inception and that are co-substantial with it. The first of these lies is the pure and simple denial of this failure. This is the claim that, if one sets aside a few inevitable details, the results are "positive overall." This thesis would be laughable if it had not been maintained for more than a half century by almost all of the French "intellectuals," with Sartre as their ringleader—to the point that in France to be an intellectual means being an intellectual of the left, which only exists and is recognized under this heading. Blindness, due to deception or cowardice, the ignominious celebration of poverty and fear as a principle of government, of deportation and death: these are the intellectual qualities that give one the right to speak in France and continue to do so. The height of infamy, in this regard, was reached by the 1935 *Congrès de la Mutualité* where all of the Parisian intelligentsia—including the bourgeois, this time, with André Gide leading the parade—came to solemnly pledge their allegiance to Stalin.

Naturally, a lie as shameless as the idyllic description of permanent shortages, police violence, denunciation, and terror calls for more subtle and nuanced formulations. The "difficulties"—and there were difficulties—are said not to be due to the regime itself but to its "deviations." Since these are the cause of all the harms, it is necessary to hold even more firmly to the regime and to refer to it as an irreplaceable model, the Archetype, for every ideal social organization. If we look closely at it, these deviations do not have their source in the regime itself but in particular character traits of certain leaders, in their individual faults. It is Stalin's murderous madness that led him to flout democracy and human rights, to rely on force, etc.—even though these are the principles and dogmas of Marxist political theory explicitly formulated and affirmed by him. These principles were first applied by Lenin. Stalin and his successors took them up again in turn. This explains why the number of historical leaders who are taken over by paranoia, practicing the cult of personality and mass assassination, has coincided with that of general secretaries and other "advisors." The most recent of these (at the time that I am writing these lines) is Ceaușescu, while the first was Lenin himself. Like it or not, it should be recognized that he was the one who instituted the gulag, suppressed every form of individual or political freedom, slaughtered peasants, destroyed the economy, and ultimately gave communism the hideous face that it would come to have throughout its history.

But here is something more serious, which no longer only concerns communism. For, as strange as this observation might at first seem, *the reason for the universal failure of communism on the economic level does not merely or even primarily belong on the economic order.* It is thus necessary to take a distance from the interpretation that is first offered and that most of those who are watching the current revolutions endorse. According to this way of seeing it, if communism failed economically, this can only be due to economic reasons. Subsequently, the analysis of communism understood in its proper sense, that is as a regime that is based on the socialization of the means of production (the tools of work, factories, raw materials, etc.), is the business of economists and can be drawn from their expertise alone. From this perspective—from the point of view of economists, in other words—one will say that the cause of this failure resides in the misunderstanding of economic reality itself. Like each specific kind of reality, economic reality has its own nature with its own laws. How then could one develop a coherent and effective economic project—and, especially, the most general one of all, of instituting a new economic system—without regard for the laws of every possible economy, for example, of the relation between wages and ability, responsibility, or the amount of work actually done? What about the laws of supply and demand, etc.? As if economic activity could be anything but the actualization of these laws and relations or anything but putting them into action. "*Laissez faire.*"

The liberalism that is preached today from all sides, to be sure, regards the wholesale failure of socialist regimes as a sort of self-validation. It makes liberalism appear as the inevitable answer that everyone seeks. This liberalism is no longer the savage liberalism of the nineteenth century, with its own series of misfortunes, with its crises, with the scandalous labor of children and women, with generalized exploitation, promiscuity, sickness, and all kinds of misery. "*Laissez faire*" no longer rules on its own, when the number of interventions are increasing on every level, whether they are interventions by banks or by governments themselves. These interventions aim to stimulate or slow levels of consumption and production, to fix the rate of growth, investment, or credit; in short, they act on the development of economic processes in order to avoid the large crises that have marked the history of capitalism. What we are experiencing instead is a neo-capitalism. It is characterized by the continuous exercise of political power and its institutions over all economic affairs in order to ensure their proper functioning.

All of these interventions, however, can only be taken in relation to a reality that precedes them. In relation to this prior reality, they are presented as secondary actions that aim to influence the direction of certain natural processes that have their own characteristics and laws. Even though, in developed economic societies, they take on the form of forecasts that are expressed in long-term plans, they continue to refer back to a prior order of things. The proof of this comes from the fact that these various programs imply a rigorous knowledge of the economic laws that they seek to influence. They thus become the work of specialists. In modern forms of economic liberalism—and in its more modest titles such as "free enterprise," the "market economy," etc.—the fundamental conviction of liberalism remains. This is the belief in the existence of an autonomous economic reality with its own system of specific regulations; it is the belief that all action in this domain must be based on the knowledge of them and thus on economic reality itself. The same thing holds for the economist and his world as for the doctor and the bodily organism of his or her patient: one should only intervene when it is absolutely necessary, and one should only do so to the least possible extent. In this way, intervention does not merely presuppose *a posteriori* knowledge of a reality that exists independently from this knowledge; the intervention itself also belongs to the reality into which one intervenes. It is simply the use of its laws of behavior and the actualization of some of them.

Here the socialist project is revealed to us in its full magnitude, and, at the same time, its failure that is observed today takes on a dramatic meaning. It does not only pertain to one type of economic regime that can be contrasted with other ones; it concerns the human being itself in what has traditionally been regarded as its dignity: its freedom. That is the crucial point. In spite of certain isolated statements that are due to the scientific climate of the time in which it was born, socialism does not consider economic reality ultimately to be independent from humans and their decisions. It is only gradually, as the result of a long historical evolution in which human beings have always intervened, that the world of the economy and its laws are presented as a hostile and foreign fate, overwhelming humanity with blows that it is unable to parry or even to understand.

After a period of drought or some other natural disaster, there is now a fertile and fecund year. The products of the earth are abundant and of high quality—but that is not wealth, however. Prices collapse; the peasants are broke; their poverty is greater than in times of famine and shortage! Now, after centuries of relaxed production, groping and limited, whose mediocre results put the people at the mercy of the first difficulty encountered, there is an extraordinary rise of a new and powerful industry. It is stimulated by the progress of knowledge and the technological revolution to which it gave rise: the appearance of mass-produced objects. Their qualitative differentiation, adaptation to multiple and refined uses, does not yet signify wealth or well-being, not even basic material well-being—quite the contrary! It is a "crisis": all kinds of goods and products are available in large quantities. There are also those who need and want them. But, these goods and products do not pass into their hands. Those who have produced these goods are unable to acquire or buy them. What a strange reality for those who live through such contradictions. What a strange economy!

Historically, socialism was the metaphysical affirmation that this reality could be changed, that all of the forces and laws that hold humanity under their yoke and have always plunged them into misfortune, in modern times more than ever, that economic reality could in some way be dissolved, dismembered, broken down, and then recomposed and reorganized in such a way that its effect on the lives of men and women would no longer be shortage, unemployment, and anxiety but rather the possibility and opportunity for everyone to be themselves. This decomposition of economic reality had to take on two aspects. It was, first of all, a decomposition by thought, by an analysis of it. Based on the results of its analysis and thus based on itself, thought could then go on to reconstruct economic reality in order to turn it into a source of prosperity and well-being. This marks the possibility of changing economic reality through thought and thus of affirming the freedom of the human being in an exemplary way. The human being is capable of mastering, rather than undergoing, the process of production on which his or her daily existence depends. That was the extraordinary and grandiose project of socialism. The failure of socialism is the failure of thought in its attempt to organize the activity and lives of human beings in a rational and efficient way. This terrifying failure calls into question the *humanitas* of the human being insofar as this resides in its thought and its freedom.

But, the question might be formulated in a more precise form that is less disturbing in the sense that it would not call into question thought as such but only a historical and particular manifestation of thought, a specific type of philosophy. One could then ask: *What thought*, by denying the autonomy of economic reality and claiming to reconstruct it in light of intellectual schemas constructed by thought, is responsible for the economic failure of socialism?

The answer is unequivocally clear: it is Marxism. That is, a cohesive group of theories has led to the economic catastrophe in the East and the USSR; it has given rise to the political upheavals that are mesmerizing the West. This catastrophe has always existed, however, in Peking as in Moscow, in Phnom Penh as in Baku, in Haiphong as in Budapest or Bucharest, in all these unfortunate countries, whether for the Khmers or the Laotians, the Hungarians or the Polish, the Azerbaijanis or the Armenians. Beyond their struggles and hatreds, communism inevitably gave rise to the same disastrous consequences for all those who aspire for their own free development and happiness, for all those who are alive.

In the first part of this book, it is thus a question of clearly recognizing Marxism as the principle behind the economic failure of communism. This principle is the devaluation of the individual. The individual is replaced by a series of abstractions that are unable, given their nature, to produce any "real" action whatsoever or of "working." One can then understand how every regime that places an abstraction of this kind at the source of its social organization—a class or a party—is condemned to powerlessness and to the destitution that inevitably results from putting out of play the only true force, which is the force of the individual. On the political level, the consequences of this theoretical devaluation of the individual are equally terrible. They are called the negation of human rights, suspicion, arbitrariness, deportation, and even death. With this situation of latent terror that ideology can no longer hide, Marxism rejoins the worst regimes that our time has known: it is nothing but a variety of fascism.

Once the cause of evil has been detected, it should then be easy to advocate for a type of regime that escapes from it by definition: liberalism. It claims to call on the energy, the initiative, and the liberty of the individual. Does not "free enterprise" reproduce the freedom of the individual? Does it not derive its own dynamism and vitality from the freedom of the individual?

The term "enterprise" is inscribed unfortunately in an economic world which is, first of all, the world of the market economy and secondly the capitalistic economy. Just like Marxism and every economic theory in general, the first of these theories—the market economy—is also the work of thought.

It is an archaic thought, one almost as old as humanity, but it is a thought all the same. It kills life and its living determinations in order to replace them with a constellation of dead abstractions: value, money, capital, profit, interest, etc. These abstractions and their many variables have taken the place of living individuals, with their desires, passions, and deep needs. Other laws than those of life, henceforth, guide the world.

Capitalism, to be sure, retains an essential relationship to life to the degree that it is based on the individual and the individual's work which it uses and "exploits" as much as it can. This is what has provided for its most brilliant successes and its unlimited power to change the face of the earth. When capitalism is presented today as the sole recourse in response to the failure of socialism, however, one forgets that, underneath its illusory exterior, it is itself in agony. For the still hidden but decisive event of our time is that this capitalism in reality is giving way to an entirely different phenomenon. Galilean technology takes over the real process of production; it gradually but inevitably discards living work, or what Marx called "subjective labor power." In a paradoxical but inexorable way, capitalism is thus eaten away by the same evil that led socialism to its ultimate demise: the elimination of subjective life and the living individual. The theoretical errors of Marxism correspond with the triumphant world of technology, which unfolds according to its own temporality and carries out the same monstrous process that casts the human being outside of the world and the world outside of life.

East and West are only two figures of the same death. Let's begin with the figure whose truth has just been revealed by history and slides into the past right before our very eyes. We will then turn to the second figure, which is a hideous specter because it no longer has anything human.

1 THE DEVALUATION OF THE INDIVIDUAL

Marxism has obsessed the minds of European intellectuals for over a century. Through various intermediaries—including political parties, unions, universities, and the press—Marxism has broken through the tight-knit circle of the "cultivated" public and reached the "masses" which it sought to mobilize in order to transform their lives. But it is caught up in an equivocation that must be dispelled from the outset. The term "Marxism" is constructed out of Marx's name. Marx is one of the greatest Western philosophers, and in fact he is the only one who thought about the world of economic facts in a radical way by going back to its roots, that is to the *foundation* without which this world, its laws and its problems—which are greater today than ever—would remain unintelligible. The economic sciences, in spite of their claim to be scientific and in spite of their mathematical sophistication, never deal with this foundation. They don't even have a clue about it. This explains why they remain very far removed from Marx's problems, in which they only see economic theories that are more or less questionable or outdated, when in fact it involves a return to the reality of life. Without life, there would be no economy, and all economic phenomena, from the simplest to the most complex, would remain incomprehensible.

It happens to be the case that Marxism is just as blind as modern economics with regard to the foundation of the economic phenomena that Marx perceived and established as the principle of all his analyses. This initial paradox needs to be explained. How could those who forged Marxist doctrine—Plekhanov, Lenin, Trotsky, Stalin, Mao, and all the others—have misunderstood the principle that Marx assigned to every possible economic world, regardless of its period or level of complexity? A precise answer to this question can be given which escapes from the play of interpretations. It is the extraordinary fact that the philosophical texts in which Marx developed the meta-economic foundation for every conceivable economy remained unpublished and unknown until 1927–33. They were thus unknown to all those who built the theoretical and practical doctrine of Marxism at the end of the nineteenth century and the beginning of the twentieth century. Two of these three texts—*The Critique of Hegel's Philosophy of the State* and *The German Ideology*—written in the years 1842–3 and 1845–6, respectively, were not published at the time because no publisher wanted them.[1] In either a direct or indirect way, they constitute a rigorous philosophical analysis of what Marx considers to be the only true reality and the foundation of the economic world. That world is not autonomous; it doesn't exist on its own. If it can only be made intelligible on the basis of a deeper reality and if this reality does not belong to the economic order, that is because this reality produces it and continually does so at each instant.

This reality is the reality of life in the sense that everyone understands it. It is called difficult or hard or short or, as Maupassant says, "neither as good nor as bad as we think."[2] Life was described by a mystic at the beginning of the fourteenth century in the following way:

> Among all things there is nothing so dear or desirable as life. However wretched or hard his life may be, a man still wants to live. It is written somewhere that the closer anything is to death, the more it suffers. Yet, however wretched life may be, still it wants to live. Why do you eat? Why do you sleep? So that you live. Why do you want riches or honors? That you know very well; but—why do you live? So as to live; and still you do not know why you live. Life is in itself so desirable that we desire it for its own sake. Those who are in hell in eternal torment, souls or devils, do not want to lose their lives; for to them their life is also so noble …[3]

What characterizes life, what makes it so desirable and so noble, is that it experiences itself. It thus ceaselessly suffers and enjoys what it is. This has nothing to do with the life that biology studies, which is constituted by processes that, however surprising they may be, nonetheless share in common the trait of being blind. In this sense, they are "things": molecules, acid chains, and neurons do not feel themselves and are not "conscious." In this respect, biological life differs entirely from the life that Maupassant, Eckhart, and common sense talk about. This is the type of life that Marx places at the foundation of the economy.

Marx is so attentive to what makes life be what it is, to the fact that it feels and experiences itself, that everything that turns out to lack this extraordinary property seems to him to lack sense and even to be impossible. And Marx loved everything that is alive so much that he placed on a lower level everything that lacks the ability to feel, to suffer, to enjoy, and to love. It is only death. We will see that his entire economic analysis is built on the basis of this key contrast. That is not a value judgment in any way or some vague or imprecise Romantic vision; instead it is the most rigorous name for one of the factors that enters into every real process of production and makes it what it is. For this process is really the foundation of the economy and of all economic phenomena in general. It can be divided into living work, on the one hand, and material elements, on the other hand, which include the tools of production as well as raw materials. Whereas the former is referred to in terms of life, the latter, as materials, will be affected always by an insurmountable coefficient of inertia which leaves them forever unable to play an active role in the process of production or to constitute it, properly speaking. Once again, this view is not the result of a prejudice. It is due to the fact that only living work is capable of "producing" economic reality and value, whereas the material elements are unable to do so. They could even be eliminated from this process, since they have no power to create value and since the creation of value could be pursued in spite of their absence. Life goes on without death and is self-sufficient. We will return to this key point later.

For the moment, let's underscore the two features of life that we have just encountered. First, there is the subjectivity of life. This concept means nothing but the fact of feeling oneself, that is to say, of life. All life is subjective. It begins and ends with subjectivity, to the point of being nothing other than it. Naturally, the term "subjective" should not be understood here in the trivial sense in which "everything is subjective" would mean that "everything is relative," or that everything depends on each person's way of seeing things: "for each his or her own truth." Instead of referring to the various ways in which an individual can think or to one's own point of view on things, subjectivity constitutes the most essential reality of this individual, one's metaphysical or ontological condition. It is one's being, inasmuch as this being is life.

The second feature of life is that it is a force, a productive force. That is to say that it is capable of creating something that would not exist without it. We will only later be able to see how far this creative capacity of life will go, but for the moment let's first say that life has the ability to change the natural world around it. By taking some of its elements away and by giving them a particular form, it gives rise to objects that come into existence through it. These objects are of two kinds: some of them serve the purposes of life and have been made by it with this aim. They are such things as food, clothes, buildings constructed for dwelling, for worship, etc. These are called "use values." The other kind of objects are the instruments that serve to produce the former ones but are themselves produced in the same way—they also enter into the category of "use values." Considering life as a force, in its productive power, Marx calls it "praxis" in 1845 and immediately classifies it as subjective. He reproaches materialism for having only grasped reality "only in the form of the *object or of contemplation*, but not as *sensuous human activity, practice*, not subjectively."[4] The term praxis will disappear from Marx's vocabulary and be replaced, in his economic work for instance, by concepts that more clearly underscore this dual character of life as subjective and as a force. Let us cite them: "inorganic subjectivity," "living body," "living work," "labor power," "subjective labor power," "subjective labor," etc.[5]

We then encounter a third feature of life that distinguishes it from the Romantic conceptions that contaminated Marxism much more so than Marx's own thought. For the latter, life is not a universal entity capable of being realized and of existing as a general reality. To the contrary, all life is individual and can only be actualized in this way; that is, in the form of a living individual. That is why the actualization of life in the individual obeys the law of continual reiteration, giving rise to countless individuals.[6] That is also why one only rarely finds the term "life" utilized on its own in Marx's texts. Instead, one often finds the term "living individuals"—such individuals, precisely because they are the only possible mode of realizing life, will be recognized as the sole foundation of all reality. In the *German Ideology*, they are referred to through the phrases "living individuals" and "real individuals" as the "premise of all history," such that history, in turn, can only be the history of these individuals.[7] History can only be made and experienced by them, even if it escapes from their will—at least, if it escaped them at least from its beginnings up to now, socialism tries to give it back to them in some way and to resubmit it to their freedom.

In the economic analyses that are the core of Marx's work after 1847, the term "living individual" gives way to that of the worker. Its rigorous sense is the same and can only be understood on the basis of life. The distinctive feature of the worker is living work. It is life itself in its three forms necessary for its accomplishment: subjective, active, and individual. When it is forgotten that the essence of the worker is life in the metaphysical sense of something that is of another order than the material thing that lacks the metaphysical capacity to create what does not yet exist, and when the individual is considered in a positivist way as an empirical being as occurs in Marxism as well as in every scientism in general, then one can no longer understand a single word of Marx's economic analysis. And it should be added that Marxism, which is historically a form of positivism and scientism, has not understood anything about it.

The reference to life under the heading of a "living individual" is for Marx something so evident that he was hardly concerned about justifying it. Given that individuals, as living beings, delineate the foundation of the economy, it is important to show, however briefly, why life takes on the form of an existence that is always individual. Its experience of itself, reduced to its pure subjectivity, is necessarily this one or that one. This singular experience is a living and experiencing of oneself. It includes within itself this Self that is irreducible to every other and that makes it into an Individual, in the sense of an individual Self. This is a transcendental Self which senses and senses itself, which is constantly affected by itself and nothing else, and which is nothing other than that. It has no alterity and no objectivity that can be seen or touched; instead it is what sees and touches, what takes and acts. It is not the empirical individual, as conceived by Marxism. It is only an individual understood in this other way, in Marx's sense—as living, acting, and moving—that can have the power to create and produce that is the foundation of the economy.

One must, to be sure, keep from autonomizing this living individual and from understanding it as an absolute principle. It is certainly a principle with regard to everything that it produces and especially with regard to all values, as their creator. And it is precisely in this way, as the creator of "use values" and, as we shall later see, of exchange values—or, in other words, of consumer goods considered both in terms of their material and economic reality—that the living individual is the creator of the entire economic order. But this individual who creates the economy did not create him- or herself; the individual did not put him- or herself into being. What characterizes the individual, to the contrary, is a radical passivity with regard to its own being. It first undergoes this in a suffering that is stronger than any power, willing, or freedom. It is this radical passivity of the individual with regard to itself that makes it a living being. For life consists of the experience of oneself in such a way that this experience is insurmountable. No one has the power to escape it, to let go of one's life, to put it or hold it at a distance in any way. As a living being who is radically passive in relation to itself, one cannot break the link that attaches oneself to life. This is why the individual is placed in its situation. It does create itself but finds itself in a situation; it is in some way already there for itself. It is as if its own being preceded it in a certain way, as if it were second not only with respect to what it wants but with regard to the original and uninterrupted upsurge of life within itself. To be a living being is to be precisely that: it is to be born from life, to be carried and given birth by it. This birth and upbringing do not cease; the individual is nothing but the experience of this inner upbringing which crosses through oneself. Although it has never been willed, one is nevertheless merged with it.

The metaphysical condition of the individual sketched here in rough outline—the condition of existing as a living being and thus as passive in relation to oneself—is something that Marx conceptualized in his extraordinary critique of Stirner in 1845-6.[8] This manuscript is extremely dense, and Marx elaborates the precise philosophical status of what will constitute the foundation of economics and history. It remained unknown until 1933. Up to then, Marxism had taken the individual as a negligible quantity, more precisely, as the pure effect of economic and social laws. That is why Marx's critique of Stirner, when it was at last read in a quick and superficial way, became the object of immediate disdain. Marxism saw it as the confirmation of its own general critique of the individual. This misreading is all the more facile given that Marx continually makes light of Stirner's attempt to be a unique individual, "the Ego" for whom the whole world is its own "property."[9]

A more attentive reading shows, however, that *Marx's critique is a critique of the definition of the individual as thought or as consciousness.* This is the classical definition of the individual, and in this case, it is a definition which Stirner borrows from Hegel. The traditional and banal conception of the human being defined by thought contrasts sharply with Marx's definition of the individual on the basis of life, as a "living individual." Everything changes depending on how one conceives the human being: either as a thinking subject dominating the world of objects which are reduced to being its representations, or as a living being immersed in life, submersed under it and its needs. In the former case, one will easily and perhaps inevitably arrive at the Idealist theses of which Stirner provides an extreme formulation. That is to say that the individual is the center of a world that is in some sense laid out at its feet, which its gaze embraces and dominates. This elevation (*exhaussement*) of the subject—thinking above everything else which is only an object for it—gives it an absolute freedom. All the powers in history that seemed to dominate the human being and bend it under their yoke—God, the State, the Law, political power, the economic world, and the external world—are in fact only the representations of consciousness. As a result, they depend on it and its free will. It is because consciousness considers God, the State, or the Law as higher and sacred realities to bow in front of—"holy," as Stirner says—that I actually bow before them, revere God, serve the State, and observe the laws of society.

The role of consciousness is to consider something as something, to consider this form in the dark as a tree or as the silhouette of a human being, to represent things in this or that way, to take them as good or bad, as worthy of esteem, or detestable. This is its power and its freedom. After representing God or the State as holy, Stirner's consciousness can with the same ease "regard them as nothing" and thereby free itself from all servitude to them. That is the foundation of the anarchist revolution that Stirner preaches: neither God nor master. This liberation is based on the power of consciousness to understand and to interpret the world as it does. In traditional thought, consciousness was defined as a power of representation. As for the economic world and property in particular, consciousness can choose either to respect it or not. Here again it can either "regard it as nothing," or consider the whole world to belong to it. However, if a particular thing, such as a house, is the legally recognized and actual property of another person, I will still be able to consider that I am the one who concedes this property right for the time being. Because that is ultimately what pleases me, it is a concession that I make freely. From Stirner's ridiculous conclusion, Marx draws the following lesson: the power of consciousness to represent things in the way it does only covers over its total powerlessness on the level of reality. The property that it gives away in this way and that it extends to the whole world is only another name for its destitution. After persuading himself that he is the sole possessor of everything and that he voluntarily and provisionally allows others to have the commodities that are seen through the store windows, the master of Stirner's school goes along his way with an empty stomach.

In spite of the apparent thinness of its target—the quixotic anarchism of Stirner—the critique developed by Marx needs to be evaluated. It is twofold: it is partly nothing less than the critique of thought as such, and it is also partly the critique of the definition of the human being in terms of thought. Let's develop these two points in that order.

Consciousness represents a thing as being what it is, as this or that thing—it represents this form in the dark as a tree or as a human being. Consciousness is thought. To represent a thing as this or that thing signifies: 1) to place this thing in front of its gaze, as an object (the term "ob-ject" literally means what is placed in front); 2) to posit it as an object that is not just anything whatsoever but has this or that nature, which is a tree or a human being. This nature of the object is what is called its essence. In the act of thought that consists of representing a thing as a tree, there is something more, namely the fact that, before representing something as a tree or as a human being, one first represents it implicitly as a thing that exists, as a being. This representation of the object as a being is the representation of its being, of the fact that it exists. This is implied by every representation of any thing and of any being whatsoever, whether it is a tree or a human being.

Such a definition of consciousness or of thought can be formulated in similar terms. For the power of consciousness to represent things in this or that way is also its power to give them this or that meaning. Following our example, it is the power to give it the meaning of being a tree or of being a human being, or, rather, the meaning "tree" or the meaning "human being." The analysis has shown us that, along with this meaning of being a "tree" or "human being," consciousness also gives its object the meaning of existing and posits it as a being. Thought, or consciousness, is thus this bestowal of sense which confers onto everything that it represents the meaning of being this or that thing, and, first of all, of being in general. What Marx's critique of Stirner's notion of the individual—which is to say his critique of thought—tells us is that the positing of the meaning of some thing—and more fundamentally, of its simple meaning of being in general—does not concern reality. Being is not reducible to a meaning posited by consciousness, to a sense, to the sense of being. Being, or in Marx's terminology, reality, is not reducible to thought.

What is reality, if it is not a representation of thought, if thought is unable to produce it even when it forms the meaning of "thing," "reality," or "being," if being is not a "meaning"? Here the enormous contradiction in Marxism emerges. This contradiction, by the way, is not unique to it but is shared with all forms of objectivism, with common sense and with other proud philosophies. If the representations of consciousness cannot claim to define reality, this is because reality exists prior to them. It is both prior and external to them: it is precisely external reality, the reality of the "world." This contrasts in two respects with Stirner's belief in the power to change or to arrive at the end by modifying one's representation of reality, or as he says, one's "point of view" (*Ansehen*). This reality differs, first of all, as the external reality of the material world, a world that consciousness can indeed represent or conceptualize in various ways but which in itself precedes this work of thought and is thus independent of it. It is precisely as something external to thought and independent of it that the world defines reality.

This reality differs from consciousness in a second respect. Social reality, like material nature, has its own laws. Thought is able to analyze and to recognize these laws after the fact, but it cannot arbitrarily create or modify them. This is why Stirner ("Saint Max" or "Saint Sancho," as Marx calls him) can indeed change his point of view on things, but they will not change accordingly. The property laws that he "takes as nothing" will continue to prevent him from appropriating the goods of others, except within thought alone. Property is one of the constitutive features of social reality, and social reality is neither produced by thought nor explicable on the basis of thought.

Before contrasting Marx's key insights with the objective realism defended by Marxism as well as the nineteenth century science with which it sought to accord, let's first note the extreme weaknesses of Marxism. The thesis that will be defended in this book and on which the entire critique of socialism as well as of capitalism will be based is that reality is not reducible to a representation or to a product of thought. The question, however, is to know this reality which is irreducible to conscious representations. When one replies that reality is the material world that is immediately conceived as being *constituted of objects*, one is referring—whether one knows it or not—to the power without which no objects would exist, namely, to consciousness understood in terms of thought. It is only for something like a thinking subject that there can be something like objects. In themselves "things" and "beings" are nothing of this kind. They become ob-jects placed before the gaze of consciousness only due to the structure of consciousness. It, in turn, provides the structure of objectivity and thus of every possible object. If one philosophy is unable to overturn an idealism of consciousness, it is surely a realism of the object. For the latter philosophy is simply a repetition of the former.

As for social reality and its laws, they, too, stand opposed to the attempt by consciousness to transform them by modifying its way of understanding and interpreting them, by changing its "point of view." Yet, it would certainly be difficult to explain them on the basis of the micro-physical particles that make up the material world. Basic science, the physics of particles, has nothing to say about them. The error of materialism has always been to claim that reality and social laws are prior to the efforts of thought to understand them and ultimately transform them, that they are thus external to representations in the sphere of consciousness and then to identify them with "external reality," understood as the reality of the material world. Instead, one should conceive *this social reality and its specific laws as foreign to the sphere of conscious representations as well as the material world—one should say with Marx: this reality is the reality of life.* In his terminology, the reality of history is the reality of living individuals. Social reality is a subjective praxis; it is social praxis.

We must now direct a radical critique against Marxism to the extent that it got rid of the Idealist definition of reality—which identifies reality with a representation of consciousness that is derived from consciousness—only in order to posit an objective and material reality. By proceeding in this way, Marxism remained captive to the classic Subject–Object dichotomy. This dichotomy can be formulated in the most naïve terms as follows: either the subject creates the object and consciousness determines its representations, or the object determines the subject and consciousness is only an effect of material processes. *Either idealism or materialism.*[10] Regardless of how one might answer this question—idealist or materialist—to answer the question thus posed is to lose sight of what in Marx's eyes is the essence of true reality, namely, the subjective life of individuals. This is neither a representation of consciousness nor a material reality—it is not conceivable as an object.

As for the problem of the individual, the result of this decisive theoretical error is that the critique of the individual defined as thought and of the power of consciousness to freely modify its representations of reality is taken as a critique of the individual itself. However, *for Marx, the critique of the thinking individual is only an antithesis which allows him to define the living individual in full force.* In what follows, we will first briefly indicate what the living individual is for Marx and then we will be able to see what abstract entities take its place in Marxism and how the substitution of these abstractions for life leads to the ruin of the regimes that were built on it.

2 SOCIETY AND CLASS AGAINST THE LIVING INDIVIDUAL

The living individual differs from the individual defined in terms of thought. In its relation to itself—which is a relation to its own life—there is no thought in the sense of a representation of objects or of a subject/object relation. What characterizes the representation of an object is a putting at a distance and its arrival in front of the gaze of thought. This arriving-in-front-of is representation itself. The German word *Vor-stellen*, which literally means "to put in front of," clearly indicates this. It is only due to this putting at a distance that the object is what it is, namely, something that is placed in front. It is to the extent that it is placed in front of us that it can be shown to us.

In life, to the contrary, this arrival of an object in front of a gaze does not happen. If we consider any of the experiences that make up our life—for example, pain or suffering, or more concretely, hunger or cold—we can clearly see that thought cannot in any way put this pain or this hunger at a distance from itself and turn it into an object. If that were the case, I would be able to represent to myself some psychic contents and name them as "suffering" or "hunger," but I myself would have ceased to suffer or to be hungry. I can indeed represent my hunger to myself and consider it in various ways, as something "purely psychological," as "bulimia," or even as an "injustice" or a "scandal." But these ways of envisaging hunger, of interpreting it, understanding it, and "thinking" about it—in short, all the different representations that I can have of it—do not change anything about the pure impression of hunger. Its being derives from a living and suffering subjectivity. This powerlessness of thought with regard to life and its various modalities is due to the nature of life. Between life and itself, there is no distance, no relation to an object, and no possible object. It is precisely because life does not really have the power to be put at a distance from oneself that it cannot escape from itself or from its hunger, suffering, or anxiety. That is also why the ego, as the living individual, is unable to get rid of its life or to dismiss what it experiences.

Back in the days when sexual liberation was an issue, one heard women say "my body belongs to me; I can do what I want with it." This way of speaking is deeply misguided because my body is not really my "property" in Stirner's sense. That is, it is not an object that my thought can represent in any way it wants to, for example, as "something that belongs to me and with which I can do what I want." The nature of an object is that it is separated from me. This characteristic of objects is found in the legal object in the sense that I can "alienate" it: sell a good that I own, donate it to a third party, put it in a trust fund, etc. Social relations presuppose that the object is naturally separated from me and thus alienable. This is not the case for my *living* body with which I am identified in such a way that its suffering is my suffering and its effort is my effort. I am unable to take any distance in relation to it or to separate myself from it by selling it. Or, as Marx bluntly says about the self, I am unable to "sell it off" (*bazarder*). This way of being riveted and thrown against oneself characterizes the living individual, and it helps to explains why, whenever the worker has to sell his body or his subjective ability to work in order to live, it is in fact he himself that he will sell—and he will go to the factory.

Why does the worker now come to sell himself, to sell his body, his ability to work, his own life? Without doubt, it is due to the obligation to satisfy the many needs that assail life. These needs are called material or natural, but their genuine sense is missed as long as one believes that it is possible to restrict them to a merely empirical enumeration. Needs for food, sex, and other things point back to a nature—in this case to a body—that is interpreted as an empirical and natural given. But what cannot be explained in this way is the character by which each of these needs is precisely a need, *lived and experienced as such*—this is its irrepressible, constraining character, the power that it ultimately has to initiate actions that aim for its satisfaction. How, then, is need experienced and lived as such? How is an action inscribed within it in such a way that it is only the extension of a need? This is something that can only be understood in terms of the subjectivity of need and its immersion in life. It is only to the extent that life separates itself from thought—from every representation, every form of objectification and every possible object—and cannot separate from or undo itself, that its various modalities such as hunger, cold, and libido can be found in this condition. Life thus does not have the time to relate to them through thought, by conferring a sense onto them and by considering them to be inevitable experiences, for example as natural necessities that have to be accepted, as a malediction tied to the "misfortune of being born," or as an "unbearable" burden. Hunger, cold, and the libido, however, are not "unbearable" in virtue of a judgment or evaluation made by thought, but because that is their nature. They are subjective in a radical sense and in the depths of their being. They cannot be put at a distance, and one cannot escape from whatever might be oppressive about them.

In life, the sickness engendered by need never ceases to grow. It changes into an overpowering suffering that aspires to put an end to itself through its immediate suppression. This movement, born from suffering that pushes it to suppress itself on its own, is a drive. It is important to understand clearly what engenders the thrust of this drive. It is, as we noted, because the suffering of need has become too strong; it is the weight of this suffering. But the weight of suffering is not due to its intensity or to the intensity of need. The weight of suffering is due to its subjectivity, to the fact that one is driven back to oneself without being able to take a distance from it or to get rid of oneself. This immersion of suffering within itself without any outlet or any way to flee it accounts for the ultimate burden of suffering. What is intolerable about it is the pressure that it exerts on itself in the experience of oneself, and it is this pressure of suffering on itself that pushes it, if not to escape—that is impossible and this pressure expresses nothing other than this impossibility—at least to change itself.

The thrust of the drive coming from suffering pushes it to change itself under the weight of the pressure that suffering constantly exerts on itself. This is the original union between the affect and action. The principle of this union resides in the tireless activity through which life works to transform the sickness of unsatisfied need into the well-being of satisfaction. The place where this thrust is exercised is the body, the subjective body of the living individual, such that the action that extends this thrust and obeys it is itself subjective and living. But the work of life that is pushed by the weight of its suffering and tries to trade this for well-being or pleasure—that is work. This is the one who is at work in the "economy," and the one whose ups and downs are recounted by history. It is thus the individual—the living individual—who is at the basis of society and history. As a living being, one carries this suffering and this active essence of life within oneself. This constantly produces a society that is nothing but its own life, that is, an activity without beginning or end in which each life is raised each time to the level of the demands of its suffering and its desires and faces them. It is because life and the individual are that way that society is what it is. It is a society of production and consumption. And that history is what it is. It is the diverse and successive ways in which human beings, over the course of centuries, have tried to answer the questions of pathos under which life continually crushes them.

To posit the living individual as the principle of society and history is not to postulate the existence of an isolated individual, like some Robinson Crusoe on the basis of whom everything would begin. This abstraction of an individual alone in the world, who would develop entirely on his or her own, is incompatible with the concept of an individual defined in terms of life. In life, individuals are born in countless numbers, because each time that life experiences itself is necessarily a singular experience. Through this feeling of itself, it engenders someone who is a Self. To posit the individual as the principle of society and history is to affirm that the reality from which society and history proceed is actually a reality like the one that the individual inhabits and that makes it a living individual. *The thrust of this endless reiteration of desire and need gives rise to the production that aims to satisfy them, a production haunted by subjectivity which is subjective like it.* What matters is thus to understand the nature of this production, that is to say, to understand it as an action seated in the living body. Its modalities are those of difficult or enjoyable effort; production is subjective, individual, and a pathos, just like the life which it extends and whose drive it carries out.

If the living individual, as we have sketched above, is the suffering and acting individual, guided by drives and pathos, and if the living individual is the principle of society as well as the laws that govern it, namely, the general law of the production of goods and values, then this is sufficient to conceptualize that a situation where individuals no longer do anything and no longer want to do anything shake the conditions that make social life possible to the core. It puts into question the bare existence of such a society. This image is not an arbitrary one. It is a simple representation of what is happening in the Eastern bloc, right before our eyes.

What still remains to be understood is why individuals no longer want to do anything. Marxism provides the first theoretical answer to this question which takes on a tragic significance to the extent that it concerns the daily life of millions of people and moreover the possibility of life itself. *What characterizes Marxism from a theoretical point of view is the replacement of the living individual with a number of abstract entities through which it claims to explain the totality of economic, historical, and social phenomena, and ultimately these individuals themselves.* This leads to an extraordinary reversal of the order of things at the end of which the principle, the living individual, became the result of abstractions that took its place. These abstractions are the products of thought, the objects of thought. They refer back to it and would not exist without it. As objects, they are dead things in the rigorous sense of the term: life is not present in the represented contents which have taken its place. As objects, they do not feel and do not feel themselves, they do not experience, they do not suffer, and they are not animated by any drive that leads toward their happiness—in short, they do not obey the general law of pleasure and pain. They are not alive. *The objects of thought by which Marxism replaced living individuals are Society, History, and social classes.* And one can understand now why regimes built on abstractions like these can only be regimes of death, as can be seen anywhere that the communists took hold of power and Marxism became the organizing principle of society.

This claim needs to be made more precisely, to be sure, because it leads us back to the broad dichotomy between life and death which guides Marx's thought and differentiates it from Marxism. An object of thought in the proper sense is a concept, for example, the concept of "history," "society," or "social class." A concept is an ideal objectivity, and as such it is foreign to reality and notably to the reality of life. That is why it is stripped of all real or living properties: according to Spinoza's famous proposition, the concept of a dog does not bark. One could indeed reproach Marxism for making use of concepts and for speaking about productive forces, relations of production, etc. But is this not the case with every theory? Isn't a theory a conceptual chain which justifies itself theoretically, that is conceptually? Yet there is something else going on in Marxism and in the human sciences to which it is so close and which have so often inspired it. It is the belief that the reality thought in the concept is of the same kind as the concept. Like the concept, it is a general reality. Society is thus understood illusorily on the model of and in the same way as the concept of society. And just as the extension of the concept includes all the beings that correspond empirically with it (in the way that the extension of the concept of the tree includes all real trees), so too real society is covered by the concept of society. It is presented as a general reality that is defined by a set of features and that includes within it all of the beings that share the same features—all of the individuals. This society became Society: a single and unique reality whose constituents, individuals, are its mirror and reflection. It is a specific reflection because it reflects and resembles Society, just as each tree resembles the Tree. Each individual is the image of the society to which one belongs; each is a child of the times. Or rather, Society is the Whole and the individual is the part, a part which is a function of the Whole. The individual is defined and determined by it.

How is the individual defined by the Society of the times? How is the individual determined by it to the point of seeming like a mere product of it? These questions can be answered quickly, given that this is one of the commonplaces repeated for half a century by schoolmasters of every country. From infancy, or more precisely from the beginning of school, the individual speaks the language of this society, a language that is already there and in which one is immersed. This language carries a whole series of meanings and ultimately an ideology that the student breathes in and out with each word that is heard or uttered. This permeation goes so far that it would be more accurate to say that it is not the individual who speaks but rather language that speaks within the individual. It is thus the case that one acquires an entire body of knowledge along with a language, the knowledge of the society of the time. More precisely, this knowledge is what enables one to take up one's assigned place, to pursue a career, a function set out by the network of social relations that comprise the society—"social relationships"—and that results from their intersections. One will occupy a place that is predefined by society and one will be the functionary for this function. All of that is so simple and clear …

For Marx, society does not exist. This seemingly paradoxical thesis is stated with an irresistible force once one reconnects it with the fundamental intuition of his thought, namely, that reality resides in life and only in it and that, moreover, this life only exists in an individual form, in the form of living individuals. Afterwards, it becomes evident, not through a naïve evidence that only looks at the surface of "things" and does not understood them in themselves, but through the metaphysical evidence which Descartes speaks about. It is an inner knowing of their reality. It then becomes evident that society is only a word or, at best, a concept to designate another type of reality: the reality of the living individuals who constitute its substance. This is another type of reality than that of an ideality or a concept, since it is never the object of a regard. Instead, the reality of life is irreducible to any regard; it is crushed onto itself and succumbs under the weight of its own pathos—it is a reality like that of hunger, pain, suffering, the effort to carry something, to pick up a weight, to hit something with a hammer, or even the irresistible happiness of existing. The fact that society has no reality of its own, whether specific or general, different from the reality of individuals is what results from Marx's polemic against Stirner: "With the aid of a few quotation marks Sancho [Stirner] here transforms 'all' [all individuals] into a person, society as a person, as a subject …"[1]

It would be wrong to consider this discussion about the nature of society as if it were the result of some medieval dispute. It has a dual impact, both theoretical and practical, that refers directly to the events that we are observing today. On the theoretical level, the thesis that society constitutes a specific reality, different from that of individuals, means that there is necessarily a change of levels in passing from the one to the other. One jumps in a sense from one qualitative level to another one. It follows that the laws of society and of social phenomena are different from the laws pertaining to individuals themselves, for example the laws of their minds. A claim like this one is made, for instance, by Durkheim and his school. It has been stated by him not only to be an essential sociological law but *the founding principle of sociology itself.* For it is only if society constitutes a *sui generis* reality, structured by a system of rules that are absolutely its own, that one could institute an autonomous discipline with its own structures and laws and with its own domain of objects irreducible to any other domains. Durkheimian sociology, as is well known, was greeted favorably by Marxism due to the similarity, even the sameness, of their fundamental hypothesis.

From this thesis, another consequence follows that is of direct importance to us. If society is constituted by a system of regulations that are heterogeneous to those whose source is in the subjective life of individuals, then between these two systems of regulations—those that are social and collective and those that are individual and subjective—a more serious dissymmetry is introduced: a difference of weight. The individual, with its infantile desires and its disappointed aspirations, seems quite fragile in comparison with the great power of society whose imperatives—to work, to act in a way that is strictly determined by it, and, first, to speak its language, to undergo its teaching, its ideology, etc.—are imposed invincibly on the individual. This social pressure is so strong that one comes to doubt whether, in face of it, any properly individual reality can remain, as a domain where the individual would be at home. Psychologists themselves have been led to recognize the presence of norms and social representations in the mind of the individual, and this occurs through an internalization of the collectivity's ideals. This internalization, for instance, is the origin of the Freudian superego, which means that the imperatives of society become those of the individual, whatever prejudices might result for the individual.

With an extraordinary violence, Marx rejected in advance the well-known theses that we just restated. He does not only deny the reality of society as an autonomous, substantial entity; he draws decisive consequences from this denial. For, if the *reality* of society can be broken down entirely into the living subjectivity of the individuals that comprise it, then the laws of society can only be the laws of these living subjectivities. These laws pertain to the continual reiteration of desire and drives as well as their successful, deferred, or failed satisfaction—the laws of a history whose principle is affective. These laws, like the history that they determine, actually have no relation with the laws of an objective reality that is external to the individual, like the society of Durkheim or the Marxists. In his polemic against Proudhon, Marx challenges the existence of society as a reality posited beyond individuals and independent from them, guiding them in virtue of its own norms for which they, consciously or not, would be its playthings. Immediately after that, Marx rejects the absurdity of this notion that society could follow other laws than those originating in the individual: "M Proudhon personifies society; he turns it into a *person, Society*—a society which is not by any means a society of persons, since it has its laws apart, which have nothing in common with the persons of which society is composed, and its own 'intelligence,' which is not the intelligence of common men but an intelligence devoid of common sense."[2]

Let's now consider the practical effects of the sociological-Marxist illusion that is denounced by Marx. It consists of a double movement that elevates society and then devalues the individual. At the end of this movement, reality is transferred from the latter to the former. The relation that is introduced between them can no longer even be interpreted as a relation between a Whole and a part. Such a relation would at least presuppose the homogeneity of the two terms, since the part is of the same nature as the Whole and for that reason must exist. Individuals, however, are no longer inscribed in the social totality in this way. They are no longer situated on the same level as it but at a lower level: they are no longer the members of this totality but its products. For society has different laws from the laws of individuals and thus another reality than theirs. And this reality is the true, actual, and effective reality all at once. It is society that acts and leads to action. It is what carries everything, and individuals are only floats bobbing on the surface of the sea.

A whole practical ideology is bound up with this conception of the relation between Society and the individual as a causal relation, and the radical determination of the individual by Society. Whether it is a question of carrying out any sort of action—either particular or general—of changing a state of affairs, or of struggling against alcoholism, drugs, and delinquency, one should always act on the true cause, on the true reality, on the Whole, on Society. The consequences—the changes in the particular behavior of individuals—will follow naturally. This occurs because their behavior was always already the effect of a determinant social state. Given that the social state was the way it was, the behavior of these individuals could not be any different from what it was. It is because society is bad that individuals are bad; it is because society is corrupt that each of them falls prey to corruption, etc.

It is helpful to note that a fortunate opportunity allowed Marx to ridicule this sociological-Marxist thesis about the primacy of society, which is not only the principle of communist regimes but also enters into the socializing ideology of Western democracies. Ironizing the theory of the "true socialists," Marx writes that "we are learning that society is depraved and consequently that the individuals who form this society suffer from all sorts of maladies." Marx immediately offers the reason why this thesis is absurd. It consists in the fact of hypostasizing society and treating it as a reality that is superior to individuals and that determines their mode of existence. Marx continues, "Society is abstracted from these individuals, it is made independent, it relapses into savagery on its own, and the individuals suffer only as a result of this relapse."[3]

The sociological-Marxist theory of the primacy of society led the regimes that were built on its postulates to choose modes of action that always bear on society itself, that is to say, on a general and abstract reality or on structures and the constituents that one had been led to recognize in society In this way, they are never living individuals, even though they are the ones who define the site and principle for every possible effective action, and even though they are the aim of the various schemas through which ordinary social processes and the changes made to them are envisioned. It is always a question of taking the Whole as a point of departure and of acting on it. This conception of the primacy of the social totality as an *a priori* regulating the behaviors and fates of individuals is so powerful that individuals themselves share it. It becomes an object of faith as well as a scientific truth. As a result, the inhabitants of socialist countries have a passive attitude that leads them to expect everything from society. To them, society is the only reality and the sole principle of effective realization. It was thus up to society, in the end, to do everything: to subsidize the various needs in every domain—food, clothing, shelter, health, education, work, leisure, even the truth and everything that one must believe. By reflection on this widespread ideology, which remains deeply rooted even in the minds of the protestors, we can even more narrowly identify the principle behind the economic failure of socialism.

Marx shares the thesis defended in this essay: all reality resides in the life of individuals, and all action resides in their effort, their subjectivity and their living corporeality. As such, it becomes clear that "Society" is something different from these individuals and external to them; it is in principle unequipped for any action whatsoever; it does nothing and never has done anything. Indeed, who has ever seen society digging a hole or building a wall, fixing a faucet, or treating the wounded? It should be admitted that when society is recognized as the only reality and the only effective power, when it is charged with organizing social activity and carrying it out, such a regime is in principle destined for paralysis—and bankruptcy. The more the belief that society is everything and the individual is nothing is reinforced, the more it enters into the minds of those who define the broad options of politics, economic priorities, teaching programs, etc., the more widespread becomes scarcity. Life becomes mediocre and gloomy to the point of seeming like its dominant trait; it becomes the true face of the country where this "social" or "socialist" ideal has prevailed.

Scarcity is not a law in the Marxist or scientific sense of the term; it is not an objective regulation affecting an objective reality. In a general way, objectivism delineates a wholly erroneous way of seeing social life each time that it is in question: its error is precisely to posit action as an object external to the individual, when it its only reality is within the individual. The so-called "objective" laws of this so-called "objective" reality are only the representations of actions that are carried out by life. They are only possible as the actualization of its powers, which are thus pre-formed in the subjectivity of individuals and in the non-organic structure of their living body. The objective laws in question are thus nothing other than the laws of these subjectivities.

It is thus a complete illusion to believe, under the pretext that these actions and works are carried out in conformity with certain norms that are common to them and that can be represented as objective norms, that they would be in themselves an objective type of reality. It is a complete illusion to believe that objective laws can give rise to the passage of any activity whatsoever into action, that they can guide the praxis of individuals, and that they can play a causal role in relation to them as if these individual actions would result from them. Laws produce nothing: causes, products, and effects are situated on the level of reality and on it alone. To speak about social praxis and to say—at the same time, in the same text—that this social praxis is subjective is to confer unequivocally to individuals and to them alone the role of producing the wealth—material, economic, and spiritual—of a society.[4] At the same time, it is to say where this activity ends is where scarcity begins.

Without any appearance of being an objective law, scarcity is rooted in the life of individuals, in their action or inaction, and it exerts its effects there as well. These effects are lack, need, hunger, cold, shortages of useful products, medicine, books and ideals. They culminate with the elimination of one very simple thing that allows one to live, namely, hope. Despair, in its connection to material misery, characterizes the situation which has been imposed on all socialist countries. One can indeed characterize this situation objectively—since one has grown accustomed to referring to the truth with this word borrowed from scientific language. However, it only has reality in the subjectivity of individuals and in reference to them.

To hypostasize society, as an object of thought and science, and to discuss endlessly the dialectical structure of this rational entity and its internal contradictions—in short, to posit it as an ideal entity beyond living individuals—does not prevent individuals from being rediscovered at the basis of all these constructions. Along with them, it is to rediscover their needs which remain intact, urgent, and more demanding than ever. When need no longer finds satisfaction in life and in the actions through which it freely changes itself in order to suppress its suffering, all that remains is for need to satisfy itself outside of social norms and the norms of life: through violence and pillage. To pillage is to seize hold of a consumable object without having produced it oneself, or without having produced an equivalent to it through one's own labor. And one can see all too well how the lack of work can end up in theft, rape, and drug trafficking. Pillage is an exemplary limit situation. It reveals a social state in which production is conferred to "society" and regarded as its own affair. Inasmuch as work is principally individual, the production *of society* approaches zero. As individuals continue to work, nonetheless, however little that may be, "society" has no other resources than to seize hold of the products of their labor. As they too continue to be hungry and cold, they have no other recourse than to seize hold of what society just took from them. Two sectors—public and private—arise side by side, in such a way that each can only survive through the pillage of the other. This is how life is eliminated to the benefit of the abstractions that are called society, the people, history, social organization, and planning. But life returns in a savage form, as a blind principle that seeks nothing more than to seize hold of everything it cannot do without, of everything that allows life to continue to live.

It is true that Marxism cannot be confined to this abstraction of society considered as a simple and self-sufficient reality. In order to explain its general physiognomy, its differentiated structures, the meaningful phenomena that are produced in it, their evolution and their history, it undertakes a finer analysis of what seem to be the real constituents, the true agents, of society: social classes. Here we will touch on its most disturbing aspect—this is what connects it to a fascist theory.

3 MARXISM AS A FASCIST THEORY

Socialist countries do not merely offer the spectacle of scarcity. They appear equally as regimes in which the individual is called into question and in which one's existence as an individual is threatened gravely. One can undergo a whole series of wrongs—one can be laid off from one's post or profession and separated from a job which one had arrived at through one's merit or knowledge. If one is a lawyer, one will now become a bellboy in a hotel. If one is a professor, one will now be sent to move dirt in the fields or to care for pigs. If one is an intellectual, a talented playwright, one will get rid of this prestigious condition, spending time with actresses, in order to go roll barrels of beer in the cellar of some sordid factory, far from one's books. Yet, the prejudice against the individual will be even more extensive than this. One's family will be attacked. One will be separated from them, or they will be set against oneself. One's children will be excluded from the university, or even the school, because their father was a pastor. Or, instead, they will denounce him, and he will be arrested, imprisoned, deported, tortured, or shot.

In each of these cases, the horror is that one happens to be condemned not on the basis of what one has done—for the violation of a rule or for some offense calling for reparations—but on the basis of what one is. It is oneself, as such, who is guilty. As a result, the proper punishment would not be a particular penalty which brings about a particular damage or harm to oneself; instead the only conceivable punishment is the suppression of one's own being. Any attenuation of this penalty—which is absolute by right—is a sign of indulgence, an undeserved favor. The last step in this terrifying logic is ultimately as follows: to lead someone who is guilty of being what he or she is to recognize this essential guilt him or her self. That alone is the salvation—for everyone. The verdict of the judge or the behavior of the hangman is thus approved and justified by the victim him or herself. For the convict too, since it is only by recognizing a guilt that is due to one's being that one is able to escape it, like an evil that is inherent in oneself.

Many explanations can be offered of the situation that we are describing. It has been observed in all of the communist countries and is characterized by a permanent violation of human rights. The first is actually the state of scarcity in these countries. Because these countries clash with the immediate interests of life, its fundamental needs, an extremely strong reaction arises within them and almost inevitably takes on a clandestine form, that is to say the form of illegality. After all, one must eat, be warm, and clothed. In spite of rationing and numerous regulations, there will thus be a constant bending of them. A whole series of behaviors will follow: the establishment and use of a second market, the bartering of products obtained in suspicious ways, through theft and ultimately pillage. These behaviors have a dual character: they are both inevitable and illegal. Everyone thereby lives in a state of illegality and can only live in such a state. One is not suspect but guilty in principle. One's only right is to be arrested. One's only possible attitude is to give away more and more collateral (*gages*)—compromises and denunciations. One can always be denounced at any moment.

The creation of this situation of fear becomes a means of governing. When one thinks about it, it is the most powerful means of all. In the end, people who are completely unsatisfied are led to drag their feet, to do less and less, and they are inevitably inclined to doubt the institutions and the powers that place them in such miserable situations. What better way could there be of repressing every vague desire of revolt, of turning heads, or of awakening a semblance of zeal could there possibly be than this widespread fear that corrupts everything? One could be watched through any keyhole, any apartment watchman could be an informer, a friend or even a member of your own family is potentially an informer. And that is because they fear that you are one yourself and that the only means of protecting themselves against eventual denunciation is to precede it; it is to get ahead of you in slander. This is how things should be understood within the regimes that are called police states. They are not composed of two types of individuals—the police whose mission is to control and arrest the other type—but of a homogenous mass. Everyone is alone with their own fear, watching and being watched, torturer and potential victim. They experience in excess the shame of inevitably being both—the price of this fear and shame is that one is no longer a living being but a survivor.

The second explanation that can be given for the existence of a police state in the sense that we just described is *ressentiment*.[1] It is tied to the former one. *Ressentiment* is certainly a common feature of human nature. Wherever many individuals are related, one of them inevitably possesses some qualities or goods that the other one does not have. The latter experiences envy for something that he or she might not have even thought about, but in the presence of the other, it is experienced as an injustice or an offense. The spontaneous and in some sense naïve manifestation of envy is often accompanied by a complex process which consists of the reversal of values; this is really *ressentiment*. If I do not have the goods or the qualities that the other has and if I cannot acquire them, what remains for me is to declare that they have no value. They are neither goods nor qualities; instead they are sins, flaws, and wrongs. Such realities are not positive but negative; they are not values but anti-values. And in cases where the intrinsic positivity of these goods or qualities can hardly be denied, it is how they were obtained that will be contested for sure. The property of this house is the usurpation of another's work; this individual's talent is the product of the socio-cultural milieu, a milieu from which another was excluded. Qualities and goods are not only objects of longing but reasons for condemnation.

Scarcity exacerbates *ressentiment*. Like a sea that recedes and uncovers rocks that had been hidden up to then, the ebb of social wealth reveals the remnants of well-being and satisfaction underneath the disappeared state of abundance as unbearable privileges. In a general way, scarcity maintains a very unique relationship with wealth, or whatever remains of it. Wealth is constantly produced and thereby constantly renewed and increased, so that everyone keeps the possibility or hope of acquiring a share of it through their own work or talents. In place of it, the nature of a regime in scarcity is such that the production of wealth is kept at such a low level that it is presented as a fixed quantity that is stopped. All that remains is to share it. And as the available amount of wealth is low and quickly becomes insufficient, this sharing must obey a strict law of justice, that is, equality: to each an equal share of cake, to utilize the union language which here echoes its source. This is the time of rationing, regulations, searches, denunciations, and arrests. This is the society where everyone, or each home or each advantage, is placed under high surveillance—the police state is in full bloom.

The claim of equality presents itself as justice, as "social justice," but it is not tenable when it derives from *ressentiment*. It would be a matter of giving everyone an equal amount of the social wealth. Such a division of goods and values could only be just, if everyone had taken an equal part in the creation of this value, which is not the case. Some work a lot, while others work very little or even not at all. But it is especially from the point of view of the effectiveness of this work that differences open up. Between effective activity and useless hustle and bustle—whether it results from sheer force or "physical" skill, from intellectual analysis and judicious choice or not—between the competence of one and the incompetence of the other, there is a margin or even an abyss where differences of quality, talent, courage, and will emerge and separate individuals. This is why we go back once again to them. The claim that the distribution of wealth ought to obey a quantitative equality when its creation is due to countless differences is only possible in the end, if such differences are taken to be negligible, not in fact but by right—even better, if they are taken to be illegitimate. For it can indeed happen that one person's work is incommensurably more useful than the other, but why? This might be due to one's training, a high level of qualification, etc. But why, one will ask again, is there this disparity of training and qualifications? This might be due to the difference between the socio-professional contexts to which the concerned individuals belong—due to class differences.

The third explanation that can be offered about the existence of a society where human rights have been replaced by fear has to do with Marxism itself. It is not content with elevating "society" above individuals as an all-powerful reality which dominates and determines them. The concrete mode in which the action of society is exercised is only intelligible if one pursues a deeper analysis of social reality. It is precisely not, as Proudhon thought, a sort of homogenous totality whose individuals would be undifferentiated members. For here one will find a worker and there a capitalist, here a farmer and there a landowner, here an artisan and there a professor. Social relations, as a result, are not relations between individuals but relations between workers and owners, agricultural day workers and owners, employees and employers, etc. That is claimed to be the reality of society; it is not made up of these living individuals about whom we have spoken up to now, but of social classes in their irreducible oppositions. These classes shape the physiognomy of a given society, just as they guide history. Up to now, history has only been the history of class struggle, of great antagonisms, some latent and some unleashed. They explain all social phenomena, the connections between their processes and thus their history.

But social classes can only determine history and society because they determine individuals first of all. This determination is both evident and radical. Isn't each human being entirely different whether rich or poor, a superior or inferior, giving orders or receiving them, secure with oneself and one's fortune or trembling with fear about the loss of employment? Such distinctions do not define the external contours of a singular existence; they affect it to its depths, including one's way of speaking, feeling, acting, thinking, and perhaps even of loving. Here we encounter one of the crucial theses of Marxist theory. Viewed as an undifferentiated totality, society does not condition individuals; instead classes structure society. These classes make individuals into who they are. They do not merely explain one's professional behavior but also one's private behavior, one's way of understanding things, or even of understanding oneself.

That is indeed true, but one must go all the way to the end of this truth, and to do that, one must overturn it. It is hard to deny the affinity between a given individual's way of life and the social category to which he or she belongs. The theoretical illusion of Marxism, however, is to introduce a causal relation between this individual considered in terms of his or her daily mode of life and the corresponding social category. Such a relation presupposes that we are dealing with two different realities: the individual and the class. It also presupposes that the causality goes from one to the other and that class "determines" the individual in terms of all his or her qualities, properties, behaviors, and ways of thinking. The sense of this causal determination implies not only the duality of the realities that it joins together but their dissymmetry or rather their ontological inequality. Class always acts as a cause and concentrates the true reality within itself, whereas the individual is only ever its product. But, what does this ontological primacy of the cause over the effect consist of? In its analysis, Marxism reduces society to the classes which are its real constituents— the reality of classes is a copy of the reality of society. In both cases, a substantial totality exists prior to its parts and conditions them in this respect. It is no longer an undifferentiated society—the "society-person," the "people"—it is a class with its defined particularities which now constitutes social reality. But, this class controls individuals and imposes its characteristics and laws on them, as the Society of Proudhon did. It is a prior, substantial, and autonomous reality whose elements are no longer anything but interchangeable effects.

Once again, it was with an extreme vigor that Marx denounced these sociologizing conceptions that are self-evident and with which Marxism tended to identify. "With the philosophers *pre-existence* of the class,"[2] that is to say for those who, like the neo-Hegelians and Hegel himself, place reality in a universal—the ancient City, the modern State, the social class— which "pre-exists" individuals not only in an obvious historical sense but in an ontological sense. It is this State or this class which provides a given individual with the characteristics and ultimately the being that are his or her own. "The Statement which frequently occurs with Saint Sancho that each man is all that he is through the State *is fundamentally the same as the statement that the bourgeois is only a specimen of the bourgeois species*; a statement which presupposes that the class of bourgeois existed before the individuals constituting it."[3]

It is important to understand the absurdity of Marxist theory, which Marx refutes in advance. Chronology is not at stake here. Clearly, a social context does exist before an individual has either the privilege or the misfortune of being born into it. The question is one of knowing what is real, whether it is this "context" or the living individuals which "constitute" it. If one considers the characteristics that define a social class—the precarity of its existence, the nature of its work (for example, manual), shelter, modes of transportation, and its forms of leisure or their pure and simple absence—one can see that *the reality of each of these "social characteristics" is a concrete modality of individual subjective life and can only exist in it*. This is the case for the malaise of need, for the "living work" which always refers to a subjective activity, and for the effort experienced by a suffering individual to have "shelter," "transportation," and "leisure." Each of these signifies a "way of being," a way of feeling good or bad, in accord or disaccord with the deep being of the individual. As for the most general traits which characterize an entire class—the uncertainty of work, the fear for tomorrow, a feeling of confidence or superiority—what do they refer to, if not to the fundamental affective determinations of life, to the individual's ownmost and deepest essence?

How, then, does one arrive at this odd representation that these characteristics, which actually draw their reality from individual subjective life and do not exist outside of it, would instead determine the individual from the outside, like a foreign substance with different laws from those of life? The source of this illusion is precisely representation. Society is nothing other than the intersecting of these activities. But, when thought tries to understand the multiple subjectivities whose combined activities form social praxis, it represents them to itself and isolates certain traits of them. They are given subsequently to thought as objective contents or as "social characteristics." The laws of subjective activity—the laws of life—are now offered as objective regulations connected to these objective characteristics. There is a great temptation to take them as the cause of subjective activity, although they are only an image of it, their irreal double. As a result, the subjective motivations and actions of life are replaced by structures and objective laws which together define a class. Class, as a simple representation of vital determinations, becomes the principle underlying them, instead. Hence, the French peasant in the nineteenth century does not belong to the peasant class because he works and plants, confronts the hardships of the seasons, and lives with his family on a plot of land that; instead, it is because he belongs to this class that he stands out in the winter mud and harvests in the summer, cares for cattle and cuts the grass! Class does not result from the specific activity of a group of individuals, from what they do and are in their daily life; it is this life, these activities, these needs, these passions and these fears that result from class and its properties! "Here again," exclaims Marx concerning this inverted genesis, "the matter is turned upside down."[4]

It is remarkable that Marx himself provided the theoretical explanation of this illusion. First, he affirms that the subjective determinations of individual life—what he calls "personal conditions"—constitute the reality of social determinations: "*in the bourgeois class, as in every other, it is only personal conditions that are developed into common and general conditions*."[5] As a result, the common or social conditions have no other reality than what is drawn from the life of individuals, and the connections between them cannot be of another order than those prescribed by life. In addition, Marx tries to explain the strange split through which the interior conditions of life and its modes of accomplishment are separated all of a sudden; they are placed before life and appear as objective conditions that are imposed on it and constrain it from the outside. It is thought which produces this split. It produces the illusion that the set of social conditions are objective conditions connected through necessary relations just like the conditions that they determine: " personal and social relations thus had to take the form—insofar as they were expressed in thoughts—of ideal conditions and necessary relations …"[6]

Once social conditions are identified with ideal conditions tied together through necessary relations, once social conditions are no longer the expression of a subjective praxis that is essentially individual, once this primary reference to life is forgotten and social conditions become understood as representations external to what is alive, once these conditions are treated as an objective autonomous reality whose structures determine the existence of individuals instead of representing them, then this absurd theoretical turn gives rise to a dangerous situation for all forms of objectivism. Since these objective conditions and their laws come to constitute reality, social science comes to have no other object than reality so understood. By becoming the object of science and the only object worthy of its research, this objective reality receives an excess of evidence. Its objectivity now becomes reality.

But social science is not a totally disinterested or useless science. Every project seeking to change society with the goal of making it better must be based on social science and its scientific results; it must be objective like the reality that it studies, so that it doesn't get lost in the fog. In order to establish a socialism that is "scientific" and not "utopian," it will have to be based on such a science and to accept its postulates, methodologies, and conclusions. The point of departure for its reflection—the reality on which it should work in order to be guided in its desired direction—will be the reality of classes thus understood; classes are the substance of society as well as of history. History itself will become scientific. This means that the action that human beings continue to exercise over events in order to make them conform to their aspirations is possible. It results from rigorous analyses, the famous "concrete analyses of concrete situations," which are concerned essentially with social classes and the power relations established between them at each moment of history.

These class relations happen to be simplified remarkably in modern times. Throughout various modes of production, they tend in effect to point back to a single opposition between those who own the means of production and those who are made destitute by them and have nothing to offer but their brute force. The former exploit the latter, of course. In exchange for their work, they are only given a part of the value that is produced, while the owners keep the other part from themselves. This is the surplus value that accumulates in the forms of huge profits and huge reserves of money. Class struggle thus gradually becomes a struggle between two classes to which all other classes are reduced; it is a struggle between capital, which Marx calls the bourgeoisie, and the proletariat. As History advances little by little and a set of social energies are invested, whether they want to or not, in these two colossal powers which face each other, the struggle takes the form of a huge confrontation.

In spite of the scientific character of the analysis that demonstrates the whole objective, social and economic, process that fuels this struggle, it takes on a hidden ethical meaning. On the one side, there is a blind and frenetic power of exploitation, while all kinds of misery exist, on the other side. The antagonistic relationship between these two powers turns out to be identified henceforth with History and in terms of two social classes, one of which incarnates Evil and the other Good. If the reality of individuals is reduced to the reality of the classes by which they are defined, then the need to suppress capitalism, that is to say the bourgeoisie, also signifies the need to suppress all members of the bourgeoisie. This is the inevitable result of the thesis that everything that exists, exists through the class to which it belongs. It exists as an "exemplar" of a class, for instance, of the bourgeoisie. From that point—that is, once a given individual is a bourgeois whose being is derived from this social determination—the suppression of the bourgeoisie entails the suppression of the individual. The elimination of a class—and the process of History marching toward the Revolution and culminating in it—is nothing but the movement toward this elimination. It is also the elimination of all those who compose it, inasmuch as they draw their reality from this class and are identified with it.

The liquidation of whole layers of the population that was carried out in a number of countries at the time of the communist revolution is thus not an unfortunate accident stemming from local circumstances or the excesses of its leaders: it is a result of the theory. This liquidation must first be given its true name: genocide. Genocide exists anywhere that a population is destroyed in its entirety, without any exception. It is destroyed in its entirety because it is bad in its entirety, that is to say, on the basis of certain characteristics that are found in all of its individual members. These general characteristics must affect the individual in a way that is profound enough to be able to touch one's own being and to define it. If these characteristics are bad, then the individual is him or herself bad, at the core of his or her being. If these characteristics should be destroyed, then it is the individual that must disappear. Where does one find characteristics of this kind, spread across all the individuals of a population and determining each of them in a deep enough way to make them what they are? The answer is in the social class, as it is understood in Marxism. Taking into account the role of classes in History, their confrontation in the revolution, and the need to suppress one or more of them, it follows that genocide is inevitable. That is why these massive liquidations of the population occur everywhere that Marxism spread its shadow, and in a more implacable way than in any other type of regime. As an exceptional fact of history, they were theoretically justified and thus considered themselves to be just.

The bourgeoisie own the means of production and seize hold of a share of the work of those whom they employ. They make up the capitalist class and are relatively few in number. Moreover, their number decreases as the means of production are gradually concentrated in the hands of groups that are smaller but more and more powerful. The liquidation of the bourgeois class should thus only concern a small fraction of the population. But, those who have an interest in this liquidation, which is a condition for their emancipation, are far from understanding this fact. They are duped by an ideology that is deployed and wisely defended by the bourgeoisie: the right to property, human rights in general, freedom in all its forms, etc. They do not perceive their purely formal character, the entirely illusory aspect of the various "rights" and "liberties." What good does it really do to have the right to move and travel, if I don't have the money to do it? The "petty-bourgeois" are those who, in exchange for the minimal gains claimed by the big bourgeoisie, share these ideals. They become the defenders of laws that the bourgeoisie has put into place and ultimately of the whole system from which the bourgeoisie is the main beneficiary.

This class is twice as miserable and powerless. In addition to the material mediocrity of its daily life, it adds a sort of intellectual and moral rubbish. It is blind to the fact that it goes both against its own true interests and those of other workers This petty-bourgeois class is numerous, in contrast with the bourgeoisie properly speaking. It is opposed to the great awakening demanded by History, the decisive confrontation between the oppressors and the oppressed that the Revolution should carry to its paroxysm in order to resolve it brutally through the annihilation of the oppressors. This annihilation will also inevitably strike out against all those who have become the objective allies of capital: its "guard dogs."

This liquidation is characterized by the fact that it is motivated by characteristics that are always general characteristics; they are common to many, or, put better, to everyone who shares them. They are the characteristics of a class. Thus, the judgment made about a class reveals itself also as a judgment about those who are defined by it and by the characteristics of it. Among these, one will especially cite education, even ahead of culture. Obviously, it is not the love of the mind that drives capitalism, at a certain phase of its development, to make the education obligatory and to diffuse culture: it is because a specific level of scientific or technical qualification of its agents was required by the system of production. What might seem like a "good"—namely, the scientific or cultural qualification of an increasing number of individuals—displays its true meaning with the petty-bourgeoisie. These class characteristics play the role of placing this class in the service of capital. Each individual who knows how to count, calculate, read, and write will be condemned to death, once one's knowledge, however modest it may be, is recognized as the indelible mark of one's true being: the individual becomes a blind servant to the world of money, thereby creating an obstacle to the Revolution, to the global and wide-scale liberation of humanity. The elimination of the bourgeoisie thus implies the elimination of the petty-bourgeois, with the exception of those who have learned to be self-critical and spit on themselves as much as necessary. They will leave behind their former ways in order to join the great liberatory movement of History and to merge into it. Another exception will be those who will come to hide their social condition, that is to say their true being, like the Cambodian teacher whose life was saved by disguising as a flower vendor.

This most formidable aspect of Marxism calls for some additional clarification. It has a family resemblance to the fascism that it has shouted itself hoarse to denounce throughout its entire history. One can only understand how Marxism is itself a form of fascism once its principle is laid bare.

4 THE PRINCIPLE OF FASCISM

I call "fascism" any doctrine that, whether admittedly or not, pursues the devaluation of the individual, in such a way that the individual becomes nothing, or else something insignificant or bad and henceforth its suppression seems legitimate. All forms of fascism thereby have an essential connection with death. We have shown that the only reality is the reality of life and that life only exists in a particular individual way. To extinguish the individual is to extinguish life in its only possible form. It is to head invincibly down the path toward the destruction of this lone reality. It is to head down the path of nothingness. Indeed, the extinction of the individual does not first or necessarily take on the extreme aspect of murder. It is most often presented as a manifestation of violence, but violence points back in any case to violence against an individual and can only be defined in relation to it. The individual and it alone is in question in acts of brutality, intimidation, arbitrary arrest, torture, or execution. Behind the various facts filling the newspaper columns of our times more than any other era, what is at stake are not the facts or events, however striking or monstrous they may be, but the metaphysical foundation of our being.

An objection naturally comes to mind. If one takes a look at the regimes which everyone labels with the infamous qualifier "fascist" and if one thinks about the most famous of them, Nazism, does one not find in the ideologies or philosophies that inspired them a reference to "life" and moreover its exaltation and glorification? This glorification is addressed primarily toward one of the most notable characteristics of life, that is its force. It thus becomes a glorification of force whose most extreme point would seem to be violence. Does this cult of force not stand at the origin of all the excesses and ultimately all the crimes for which these regimes have been found guilty?

Such objections are nonsense and should themselves be denounced strongly. In response to them, it should be stated that the glorification or exaltation of life cannot ever be the source of any kind of evil. What, then, are the crimes that can be imputed to Nazism and fascist regimes in general—including those which have not been labeled by this name but for whom it would be just as suitable as for Nazism? These are crimes precisely, in the proper and non-figurative sense of the term, in the sense of acts that have led to death. Instead of the exaltation of life being the principle of such acts, it is instead the hatred of life and it alone that can give rise to them. To connect the "philosophy of life" to the Nazi atrocities is not a simple absurdity; it is also an extremely suspect attitude to which we will have to return. Let's just say here that life as such can never be at the origin of a crime, that is to say an act turned against itself, *unless it is engaged in the monstrous process of the self-negation of the self which will be the dominant feature of modern nihilism and fascism.*

If one considers force, which is the characteristic of life that seems to lend itself most easily to the criticisms above, then here too it should be recognized that it, like any other property of life, is good in itself. For what would we be able to do, if we were without force? How could we satisfy the basic needs of life, its vital needs, if no power were there and if it were not co-present with each of these needs and co-substantial with their being? Satisfaction, that is also to say the possibility of life to continue to live, comes from the use of this power and from it alone.

The relation between force and life must, however, be understood on its deepest level. As such, force no longer only appears as a characteristic of life but as its essence. Indeed, force cannot be considered separately or apart from need, movement, seeing, the will, intelligence, or love. But instead, there is a force of need, of seeing, of intelligence, and of love. Without force, each of these properties that are gladly recognized in human nature would be nothing, not even a vague desire. Even it implies at least the idea of a force which would allow it to accomplish what it seeks to do.

Why is force spread out across all of the properties of life as what permits them to exist? This can be understood easily by considering the action of the simplest force: the force by which I move my hand and fingers in order to take hold of an object. This force could never be exercised, if it were not already in possession of itself and able to make use of itself. This condition in virtue of which every force has always already taken hold of itself—for example, this immersion of our body and each of its powers in oneself—is the greatest force. It is the force of force but also of weakness, movement, intelligence, wanting, desire, and love. This greatest force also inhabits weakness and is what makes the weak so strong. This is why, when they are pitted against an apparently superior force—when the weak or sick attack those who are around them and care for them—they prevail over them without fail.

If we limit ourselves to the study of a particular force, we can then understand that, regardless of the specific power it is—the power to take something with one's hand, to move one's eyes, etc.—each force contains within itself this greater force that allows it to be joined to oneself, to be held, and to be kept in oneself. Every force has an essential reserve, and this is why we never see a force as well as when we perceive this reserve. Beethoven's genius is to have captured this feeling of an overpowering and invulnerable force better than anyone else. This is precisely because for him the unleashing of forces and their irrepressible rise can only occur through this reserve from which they continually erupt anew as an original and inexhaustible power. But this greater force that resides within each force and more generally in each property of our life is precisely life itself. It is life's capacity to experience itself immediately, in the embrace of pathos which lets it coincide with itself. It allows each of its powers to make use of life and to be able to act.

Let's add an important clarification. A simple force—like the force of raising a foot, of hitting something with a hammer but also of maintaining one's attention, of keeping up one's effort—can be either more or less. In this way, one individual, for example, might be stronger than another, might have a greater aptitude for concentration, etc. By contrast, the force of this force does not have degrees or variations. It is the same for all individuals, because it is absolute, unlimited, and infinite. What does the infinity of force signify in contrast with the finitude of each particular force? It means that, however limited it may be, each force is experienced in the fullness of its being, without being withdrawn or withheld, with such an intensity that nothing can break the connection by which it is linked invincibly to the self. Try, as Malebranche said, to make a circle in which the rays are not all equal. Rational necessity at least leaves us the possibility of turning our regard away or of standing at a distance. This possibility itself is a force. The force through which it coheres with the self cannot be defeated by anything. Turning our regard away from this would be pointless here, because there is no room for any regard between this force and itself. There is only the embrace of pathos, where life is crushed against the self and touches each point of its being. This is the case precisely for each force. Whatever its power may be, it is riveted to oneself without any possibility of putting it at a distance or in the background. There resides the infinity that is opposed to the finitude of each particular force. The infinity of the greatest force is identical to life.

We have shown how this life engenders each time a living individual. As the experience of oneself, it necessarily entails a "self." The fact of being oneself is what defines the true Individual transcendentally. Each real pain, for example, is inevitably a singular experience, *a* pain, *this* pain that one experiences *oneself*. The singularity of this experience signifies nothing other than the fact that, in order to occur as what it is—*as* a pain or as *this* pain—it necessarily entails a Self that is irreducible to any other one. It is in the fact of experiencing oneself, inasmuch as it actually takes place, that a singular Self is inevitably produced. It is in life, each time that it is alive, that an individual life is born.

One ordinarily speaks about "the individual" or "living individuals" in a naïve and pre-critical way. It is taken to be self-evident that they are individuals and that they are alive. They are individuals just as chairs are chairs, and they are alive just as chairs are in space. They are empirical realities that have the additional property of being alive. But living empirical realities, like molecules or cells, are not Individuals and have nothing whatsoever to do with them. One can only understand what a living individual is on the basis of the original revelation of Life within oneself, by starting from the metaphysical phenomenon of Life, and by recognizing it as the original Revelation presupposed by everything that is experienced and experiences itself.

It is essential to understand this metaphysical condition of the Individual, because fascism instinctively defines itself is in relation to it. So, it is in relation to this condition that fascism can and should be understood. Fascism always implies the devaluation of the individual and, at the basis of this desire to lower the individual, there is the desire to negate it. This negation of the individual leads fascism to appear as a force of death from the outset—but what individual is involved here? What aspect and what part of its being should be targeted, attained, and negated in order to speak of fascism here? The answer is that which makes the individual a living being. Fascism targets the individual's power to feel, to will, to understand, and to love; more profoundly, it targets one's capacity to feel oneself and this way of being a Self who is different from any other one. In other words, fascism strikes the place where the Individual is an Individual, where this singular individual exists *in its life*. And that is how it strikes the individual at the core of its being, in what makes one be who one is. It strikes the radical subjectivity in which one feels and experiences oneself as a living being. And, it is in this respect that fascism is truly a force of death.

The limit situation where the truth of fascism is revealed to us is torture. Torture appears, first of all, as a means utilized for the sake of a specific end. This usually consists of forcing a person who is presumed guilty to speak in order to obtain important information from him or her, whether this information concerns him- or herself or whether it relates to others. The means employed is suffering. It is supposed that by increasing this suffering through various procedures and making it become unbearable, the one who undergoes it will have no other desire than to make it stop, and no other means to stop it than to speak.

But in torture the means becomes the end more quickly than in other human affairs. In torture, it is no longer the possibility of recovering a network that is important, but the torture itself. Even when it only serves as a means to an end, it is chosen due to its fascinating character and its metaphysical meaning. Torture goes back to the place where the individual is him- or herself and thereby strikes at his or her core. There is life at the heart of the individual; there is a pure subjectivity where life touches itself and where the individual is immersed in its own being. This is an entirely passive experience which consists of undergoing what one experiences—in the same way as a pain is experienced and in which one insurmountably undergoes what it is. This way of undergoing is a way of suffering. Suffering is not initially a particular content of the life of the individual. It is the very fact of living, inasmuch as living is experiencing, undergoing, and suffering what one is. Suffering is only the actualization of this "suffering" that constitutes the essence of life. If torture is addressed to suffering and if its means is in reality its end, this is because it is addressed to life itself, to the individual in its life. It leads life back to its proper place, to the place where its experience of itself becomes a paroxysm, to an intensity that is unbearable. Just as Kierkegaard describes despair, subjectivity is enflamed. The capacity to feel in the sense of undergoing what one is and of suffering from it by being driven back to it without being able to withdraw or slip away, is carried to its incandescence, to the extreme point of suffering. Life is set ablaze. It burns from its own fire which is nothing other than the exaltation of this suffering that dwells within life and makes it into what it is.

But why does fascism, like despair as well as every other fundamental human experience—like Eros and like sadism—lead life back to the essence of living? Why does it, so to speak, set fire to pure subjectivity? Is this in order to give it fully to itself and to finally complete itself? Is this in order that, at the end of its suffering, by suffering what it is all the way, it might at the same time arrive at a full experience and the enjoyment of its being, at the pure happiness of being alive? It could indeed be the case that in torture, at the moment of a cry or tears, the torturers and the victims would allow one another to lift the veil that hides the deepest mystery of being. In what way, then, does fascism differ from the limit experiences where life is in touch with its Basis? *In this sense, it only sees the means of denying itself in this supreme emotion of life and of carrying out the monstrous work of negating oneself. Inasmuch as this negation must come from it and be its own deed, the negation of life is a self-negation.*

It is in the cry of suffering, the moment of denouncing a comrade, of letting go of the required information, of delivering over an entire network—and many other things beside those: it is the moment for the individual who does all that—who cedes, denounces, and accuses—to say that he is nothing, nothing but a coward and an informer. But this abomination does not only concern this particular individual; it reaches all of life. For it is only when life is fully alive, when its essence is recognized, when its subjectivity lights up and burns with its metaphysical fire, when the suffering and joy of this subjectivity are carried to the most extreme degree of their intensity, that this life confesses precisely to its ignominy.

If one examines all these specific enterprises and the various ways in which fascism deals with the individual, one will see that they all have the ultimate aim of forcing the individual to show its lowness and its indignity. The point is to establish that the individual is nothing, but it is oneself who must pronounce the verdict, affirm one's nothingness. It is in this way and only in this way that one is and truly will be nothing. In a camp, starving prisoners are reduced to rummaging through trashcans and to picking through the scraps like pigs. But it is up to them to adopt this behavior and up to them to declare that, in and through this behavior, they are no longer really human beings, and for this reason, that they no longer need to be treated as such.

Many different paths are followed by fascism in order to carry out its ultimate plan: the self-negation of the individual and of life itself. These paths can seem opposed to such a point that it becomes problematic to group these different phenomena under the same heading. If we consider the Marxist definition of the individual in terms of the class to which one belongs, can we then recognize an analogous aim to torture which focuses on the subjectivity of the individual and exalts the individual only in order to lead to its destruction? In the objectivity to which Marxism is devoted and in the theories that claim to be scientific by restricting themselves to the exploration of an objective field, do we find anything similar to the hopeless pathos of a subjectivity delivered over to self-destruction? What characterizes scientific objectivity is precisely the fact that it is built on the exclusion of everything that derives from a particular subjectivity or refers to it. As such, it would be incompatible with a rationality that consists in universality, in a field of truths independent from impressions or anyone's feelings.

But in the theory of classes, it is necessarily a question of the social properties. We have shown in detail that they are subjective in essence; they can only take place in the life of an individual. This is not due to an empirical contingency but an essential necessity. This is how, for example, one can speak about labor that is "manual," "difficult," "skilled," or "unskilled." These are all "social" properties, but they all refer back to the real labor whose reality is drawn in each case from a living body that is different from every other one. To grasp a social property in its subjective reality is inevitably to rediscover this most profound place in life where the individual is given to him- or herself as a metaphysical self that is irreducible to any other. This is the reason why Marx said that the social properties of individuals who belong to the same class are "alike." In all real labor and in all real effort, there is inevitably this subjectivity of an experience that is radically individualized.

Due to its objectivism, Marxism misunderstands precisely the singular subjectivity of each experience. To consider a social property as an objective reality, even when it is something subjective that can only come into existence as a modality of life, is to negate it. For this social property is in fact what defines the individual. To the degree that this social property gets torn away from its living subjectivity, the individual undergoes the same fate. Just as the social property became an objective determination taken in a network of relations that are themselves objective, so too the individual becomes something objective, a point of intersection of objective social relations that is determined and defined by them.

It is necessary to think rigorously about how social property, together with the individual defined by it, comes to be objective. This is first revealed (*se traduit*) by a decisive, but undetected, modification. As long as social determinations are maintained in their radical subjectivity, we have seen that they must all be similar. This is the case with respect to labor that is "difficult"—anything that is really difficult is only difficult as something that is lived by someone. But, when one thinks about the difficult character of labor or more generally about the category of "difficult labor" under which various kinds of labor could be listed, this characteristic then seems like a general, abstract, ideal entity. It becomes comparable to other entities of the same kind: labor that is "skilled," "unskilled," etc. Characteristics like these also have another feature: they are not merely similar—like the effort of two workers who are busy trying to lift something—but identical. The same mental content comes to mind for the union representatives who treat the remuneration of "difficult" labor in this way. This identity must be taken in a rigorous sense: it is an ideal but absolute identity. What this means is that, by intentionally aiming toward an ideal content of this kind, different individuals attain one *same* reality in the strong sense of the term. But if individuals are different in themselves, or similar in varying degrees, and if they aim toward an identical general reality, this is precisely because it stands outside of their subjectivity, in front of their regard.

The decisive feature by which these general, abstract, and ideal characteristics turn out to be identical is thus their objectivity. However different their individual subjectivities might be, they become identical at the very moment when the living properties of individuals are torn away from their original subjectivity, posited outside of it and placed before a regard. They become one and the same objective reality, which is out there for each and every individual. Representatives, for example, argue about the same "difficult" characteristic of labor, just as it is the same isosceles triangle about which geometers carry out their proofs.

In the Marxist theory of class, individuals are defined by characteristics that are identical and also objective. When this happens, individuals themselves are identical. This means that they no longer exist as individuals, inasmuch as individuals are different in nature from one another. This point must be maintained and reaffirmed. Individuals do not differ because they have imperceptible differences, in spite of their deep structural similarities, as is the case on the biological level for living organisms. Nor, on the human level, do two "individuals" differ because, in virtue of a particular morphology, one would possess abilities that another one would not have: the ability to run faster, to jump higher, or to understand more quickly. Individuals do not differ due to empirical particularities of this kind, where there would be minimal differences in virtue of which everyone is slightly different from the norm but yet remains within a range of possibilities. Instead, as living beings, they differ on the basis of an essential identity, on the basis of the Life within them. We have already recognized this point. One's experience of life is always a singular experience. It gives rise to a metaphysical Self that is Individual and irreducible to every other one. Individuals are not different because their properties are different or even opposed; instead, it is because they are different that their properties differ and cannot be anything more than similar. This irreducible, metaphysical Self is what fascism wants to reduce by leading it to negate itself through torture or by any other process leading to the same end. Moreover, this very same metaphysical Self is negated theoretically by Marxist theory. How so?

How does one move from singular living subjective determinations—which are naturally individual and cannot be anything more than similar—to social objective determinations that are identical? How does one come to define the individual through objective identical determinations such as those of a class? This occurs through an act of thought. By putting them before thought as properties that it can see and that are the same in this vision, thought substitutes them for what can only be experienced in a singular subjectivity. By identifying the individual with these properties that can be seen, it omits in principle whatever stands outside of vision, on this side of the spectacle, in the invisible dimension of life, and only exists in it. Should we then say that each act of thought is a murder? And, to the degree that this murder is committed against the individual itself, does thought maintain an obscure and troubling connection with fascism? This question needs to be raised at least. If there is a common-place in modern political thought, it is surely the affinity of fascism with a certain irrationality. It is tied, as if by chance, to the concept of life, and life is taken to be synonymous with obscure and uncontrolled forces. To this ever threatening irrationalism, there would seem to be no better remedy than objective and scientific thought. It draws its power of clarification and intelligibility from placing each thing within a network of objective relations that are brought to light. But, what if the opposite were true? What if one found oneself to be negated by being exhibited in this light that is believed to be the light of truth and to which everyone believes they owe their own being?

Let's consider another form of fascism, one which is usually placed under the generic heading of "racism." What is racism, if not the claim to define the individual by a certain number of objective characteristics? In this case, it is through ethnic characteristics that one can ultimately under-stand all the characteristics of the empirical, anthropological human being: biological, psychological, sociological, and cultural characteristics in the broad sense. On the basis of these characteristics, one will try to describe a certain ethnic type. This or that particular ethnicity will be placed under a type, and along with it, each of the individuals who belong to it. Schemas will be produced for understanding its mentality and behavior. They are taken to be incomprehensible on their own, but they can be clarified when one believes that they can be related to the type in question. One of the most general types is "the primitive mentality"—a topic about which a lot of ink has been spilled for over half of a century. Ethnology continues to add even more chapters to that book.

It is important to understand that racism has nothing to do with the real or supposed existence of types of this kind, of ethnic groups or of "races," a word which it would be better to avoid. That is why every discussion of racism misses the point from the outset, if it attempts to evaluate the meaning or the mere existence of otherwise heterogeneous characteristics through which one seeks to delineate a particular ethnic type. Among the characteristics that may or may not be constitutive of a specific ethnic type, it does not matter at all whether they are biological or whether they do or do not have a meaning for the type in question. *Racism exists whenever one takes a natural characteristic or more broadly an objective character-istic to be constitutive of the reality of an individual—although this reality is purely metaphysical. It consists of the singular experience that life has of itself and in which this irreducibly singular Self is inscribed each time as a living individual. In this experience one cannot find any of the properties that ethnology, racism, or Marxism speak about, because one cannot find anything objective in it and nothing objective can, in any manner whatsoever, "define" it or "constitute" it.*

It should be recognized that there is a social racism just as much as there is racism as such. Both exist for the same reason: after an objective determination is considered to be the real being of the individual, it does not matter whether this determination is social, natural, or ethnic, whether it is one's profession, skin color, gender, or age. Here one objection could be raised, however. Have not we ourselves established that social determinations in their true reality—and not in the illusory objective representation of them formed by thought—are subjective? Do we not rediscover them on the level of life? They are deployed in the living subjectivity of the individual; they get their ontological density from it. Afterwards, are they not more real than ever? It is thus correct to say that social determinations "determine" the individual at the bottom of its being—in a much more essential way than any objective property, like height or skin color. And this determination consists in the fact that they are lived, felt, and experienced by the individual as who one is. This goes for labor, for social roles, and for overall living conditions. The mistake of Marxism was simply in considering them to be objective. In their subjectivity, by contrast, do not these social determinations establish difference at the core of the individual? Do not all separations, all class oppositions, and all segregations become possible once again?

The point thus bears repeating: after this reference to the subjective reality of the living individual is posited, so too is the irreducibility of one's individuality. Moreover, all of the properties and determinations that, having been stamped by this radical individual, are also irreducible. They will always be different from anything that is experienced by another. We are indeed at the site of all differences but in a much more radical sense than thought could ever have imagined. The differences that are born from the irreducible individuality of a living subjectivity are totally different from the differences of class, even if they are grasped in their subjectivity. In such a case, there is an analogy between an objective social characteristic like "hard labor" and the "real experience" corresponding to it. But, as Marx notes, "one man is superior to another physically or mentally," and so labor that is claimed to be objectively difficult will be relatively easy for one but exhausting for another.[1] By passing from their objective representation to their subjective realization, "social" determinations do not merely change their ontological location. They are entirely disrupted. They are no longer anything but an affect, an inexpressible and incommunicable emotion of life.

Here we are reunited with an abyssal singularity that swallows up all determinations and all social particulars, where every objective criterion by which they would be recognized, compared, and even referred to disappears in the Night of this absolute subjectivity. But, paradoxically, it is precisely at this moment that we are in the presence of the only conceivable and real equality that exists between these irreducibly different individuals. This is precisely their metaphysical condition as individuals who are engendered in life as the singular Self in which life is realized each time. To be sure, we have already encountered this essential equality of all living individuals, beyond their objective as well as their subjective properties. And this was precisely with regard to the most significant of them: force.

More than any other quality, force introduces a clear inequality between individuals depending on whether it is given to them profusely or parsimoniously, as a result of any circumstantial factors such as age, gender, or any other empirical or biological characteristics which might appear as a given fact. It is on the level of immediate facts that it first becomes possible to differentiate between the strong and the weak; their struggle will then be repeated on all other levels of social relations. But, as we have seen, each force—whether it is weak or strong—is only possible through the presence of a greater force within it that already cast it into itself and put it in possession of itself. This greater force is nothing other than life, the original experience that each force has of itself and that enables it to use its power. This is the same in all individuals. They are thus metaphysically equal in what makes them into individuals. This metaphysical equality also signifies, in spite of and beyond all appearances, the equality of their ultimate force.

As for its judgment about the individual, fascism would seem to be opposed to Marxism. By exalting force, fascism claims to justify the difference between the weak and the strong. It even exacerbates this difference and is thereby based on it. But this difference is illusory. Because it is metaphysically false, it is inevitably refuted on the level of the facts. Small, swarthy women have always known how to stand up to beer drinkers. This is not because beer takes away muscle and converts it into fat, but because the same irrepressible metaphysical force resides in all living beings as the very condition of their coming into being and as the principle that engenders them at each instant.

In order for an actual difference between the weak and the strong to appear, in order for a real inequality to emerge between metaphysical equals, an extraordinary metaphysical event is required. It is necessary for the greater force—which is to say life itself—to fall ill so that it can become less for one than it is for another. Since the greatest force is always absolute, this would not be possible unless it were the case that life itself that would begin to turn against itself: only the self-negation of life, precisely because it proceeds from life itself, can reach it. This *ressentiment* of life directed against itself is what creates weakness. A difference between the weak and the strong can only be introduced as a condition of and as a result of this prior self-negation. This self-negation of life is the primitive form of death and at the same time the principle behind fascism, since the evaluation of the strong and the weak presupposes that the sickness of life has already carried out its work. Who, then, are the weak, and who are the strong? Those in whom life has not been disavowed are thus totally foreign to this distinction. They do not experience it within themselves and find it hard to see in the eyes of others.

It is a world homogenous with the self-negation of life that has produced the distinction between weak and strong, the *ressentiment* of some toward the others. This feeling, and the scent of death, is always there when life begins to turn against itself. In spite of its apparent exaltation of force and of life, every form of fascism has this scent of and taste for death, from which it secretly emerges and to which history returns it. "Long live death!" That is its true profession of faith. Hitler, when he lost, is said to have wanted to lead all his people into death with him.

But let's leave it to the dead to bury their dead. The fascist attack on the living individual has allowed us to reveal the metaphysical essence of the individual. Before observing the various ways in which the individual is eliminated from Marxist regimes as well as the democracies that are believed to be opposed to them today, it is first necessary to establish the decisive role of the living individual in the economy, that is to say, in the concrete activity of society. What the devaluation of the individual signifies—the ruin that it inevitably entails for this whole society—will then be shown to us in more precise and more terrible evidence.

5 THE LIVING INDIVIDUAL AND THE "ECONOMY"

Defined in terms of life, the individual is presented as a force, and this force is the principle of the entire economic universe. In this universe, force is called "labor." The nature of labor can thus only be understood on the basis of the nature of force. Force is just another name for labor. Like force, labor is subjective and living; it is rooted in life and is only produced in life. It is only real in this way. Subjective labor, living labor, and real labor are equivalent terms.

Living labor is the principle of the economy in two ways. Under the heading of the economy, one can include the set of activities through which humans produce the goods that are necessary for their survival and development. This production consists of transforming the elements of nature so that they conform to human needs. These are "use values," which thus include the totality of "products" that are consumed. The force of life is what brings about this transformation of nature in order to make it suited to human needs—this force gets called labor when it is exercised for the sake of this end. Given that the history of humanity is the history of the human transformation of nature, the economic universe is coextensive with this history. Its substance is thus the force of life; it is living labor.

The economic universe does not consist merely of the production of use values: it implies the exchange of them. A human group that primarily produces wheat will seek to obtain, in return for its surplus, goods such as oil, wine, or artisanal objects. How, *in what proportion*, is it possible to exchange wheat for oil, tanned hides, or cloth? The possibility of exchange is surely the first major theoretical problem confronted by humanity. It is an urgent problem, like the needs that it extends and in which it situated—this problem is both posed and answered by life. The objects of need, though qualitatively different, are nonetheless all the products of labor. The exchange of these objects comes down to the exchange of labor, and exchange is only possible in this way. Different amounts of different useful objects require the same amount of labor. For this reason, they will be considered to be equivalent, *in spite of their quantitative and qualitative difference*: x number of objects A will be exchanged for y number of objects B. The proportion by which one object can be exchanged for another one—*its exchange value*—is thus determined by the amount of labor it involves. When it enters into exchange and is measured in proportion with the amount of labor involved with it, a use object becomes commodity. The more labor involved with a commodity, the higher its value. When two commodities include the same amount of labor, they are equivalent and can be exchanged for one another. Exchange—the "circulation of goods"—is based on this law and always obeys it.

After positing the possibility of exchange, it then turns into its opposite and seems like an impossibility, an *aporia*. It has been said that two commodities can be exchanged, when they have been produced by "the same amount of labor." But the labor that produces actual goods is subjective and living labor. In the night of subjectivity where force is deployed, there is no object or measure, no light can clarify the relation of labor to the goods—there is nothing that can be measured. The power of living labor is never revealed in any other way than in the pathos of its effort. But this pathos is no more measurable than the "taste" in one's mouth or the intensity of love. If the exchange of goods is the basis of society, and if this exchange is nothing other than an exchange of the real labor that has produced them, then its possibility slips away at the very moment that one believes to have grasped it.

It is important to be cautious at this point. The impossibility of exchanging labor—that is to say, subjectivity—does not present a difficulty internal to the economic universe; *it is the decisive fact that gave birth to this universe and made its invention necessary*. The economic universe is an invented universe; economic reality is an invented reality. What does this invention consist of? Since it is not possible to measure the living force that creates use values and since such a measure is what permits them to be exchanged, the only solution is to replace this unrepresentable and unquantifiable subjective activity with an equivalent that can be measured—with something quantifiable and calculable. This equivalent will necessarily have two characteristics: 1) in contrast with the power of living labor buried in the pathos of its subjectivity, this equivalent will need to be objective; and 2) by stripping away its reality along with its subjectivity, this equivalent will only be a representation of this force, its irreal copy, its "idea." *The economic universe is the set of objective equivalents—irreal and ideal—that have replaced the real power of living labor so that it can be measured and counted. They exist instead of and in place of this ungraspable force.*

Now we can draw up an initial list of these ideal objective equivalents to labor power. These equivalents constitute the fundamental concepts of the economy. The first one is "abstract" or "social" labor. It is a representation of real subjective labor, and this representation is henceforth one of its irreal and ideal characteristics—like the social characteristics comprising "social class," "manual labor," "skilled labor," or "unskilled labor," etc. These characteristics allow for a qualitative evaluation and thus an initial comparison of labor and consequently allow for a comparison of the goods produced by them. But exchange requires a quantitative evaluation. This comes from the measurement of the objective length of labor. This measurement becomes possible through the fact that objective duration replaces the lived temporality of labor, and it is composed of equal units—hours and minutes—that can be counted. The goods that result from the same social labor (a quantitative identity of the number of labor hours and a qualitative identity of the type of labor involved) will have the same exchange value. They will be able to be exchanged.

Clearly, the exchange value is the representation of the use value of an object that has become the commodity of the social or abstract labor that it contains. This abstract and social labor is itself a representation—a quantifiable, irreal copy—of the real labor that actually produced this object. The exchange value is thus the social labor reproduced in the commodity-object. Social labor is the objective, ideal equivalent of real labor; it is a quantified, irreal copy that is supposed to represent it. Money, in the end, is nothing but the exchange value captured in its pure state. A certain amount of money is always the representation of a certain amount of social labor. Whereas the exchange value represents the amount of social labor in a useful object or a commodity, money represents this social labor in itself. It is not invested in any object whatsoever.

From this quick overview of the fundamental concepts of the economy, the results are as follows:

> Contrary to Marxist dogma as well as common sense opinions, *economic reality is not a reality: it is neither the reality of the living individual nor the reality of the material world.* Economic reality is constituted solely out of ideal entities that are never anything but the irreal representations of something that belongs to another order: the living subjectivity of individuals, their force, and the force of nature. To echo Marx, there is not an atom of matter that enters into the "reality" of exchange value. Economic reality is entirely non-material.

Conversely, as for nature and more profoundly the subjectivity of living individuals, their reality is entirely foreign to economic reality. The deployment of the subjective powers of one's living body—for example, to walk, run, breathe or even to suffer, love, think, imagine—is not economic at all. Likewise, all kinds of things—stones, trees, the air, or the sea—have nothing economic about them either. This is why it is necessary to delineate unequivocally the relation between life and the economy and to understand them through their complete heterogeneity. Economics stands outside of reality; reality stands outside of economics.

If the economic collapse of socialism is to become fully intelligible, what needs to be shown is the following: even though it is foreign to the economy, the reality of living individuals is nonetheless its sole foundation. The force of these individuals produces all economic determinations and continually produces them. An obvious fact stands out here: if this force is weakened or disrupted, then the foundation of the entire economic world is shaken. To the extent that this world remains the condition for the maintenance and development of life, and to the extent that the exchange of consumer goods is one of the conditions of daily life, this world itself is attacked at its core and faced with the threat of death. By drawing from Marx's theses and applying them to capitalism as he did, we are going to establish how the force of the living individual produces the entire economic world and produces commodities with exchange values. Initially, capitalism will be taken only as an example, such that what holds for it will also hold for socialist regimes. We will then see, in a striking way, how it is actually the individual who does everything in any economic regime whatsoever.

Every process of production is twofold. It develops on two levels that must be carefully distinguished so that one does not slide into confusion, as economists usually do. It is partly a real process and partly an economic process. As a real process, it contains two types of elements. First, there is the subjective force of individuals, their living labor; it is this force and it alone that is productive. Second, the real process also includes the tools of labor as well as raw materials; unlike the labor power, they are objective elements taken from nature and transformed by this subjective force. The results of this transformation are not only, as we have seen, manufactured products but also the tools of labor themselves. It should be underscored that the real process of production is not an economic process and that none of its components is in itself an economic element. They only become economic at the moment when the products of labor have to be exchanged for other products—that is, when real and living labor is duplicated by an abstract entity that can be quantified and calculated in its place. It is only then that there is an economic process of production.

The economic process of production includes all of the economic entities that replace the elements of the real process: their ideal, irreal equivalents. These include, on the one hand, the exchange value of the goods produced, the tools, and the raw materials, and, on the other hand, these exchange values in their pure form as sums of money, such as wages. By its genesis and in some sense by definition, it is evident that the whole economic process is the copy of a real process, just as each component of this economic process is the copy of a component of a real process. To show that in a capitalist regime, for example, it is the living individual who does everything is to show, first of all, that the production carried out in the real process and the action involved in this production is the action of the individual. It is identical to and coextensive with the individual. Second, it is to show that all of the economic determinations that constitute the economic process are themselves produced by the living labor of the living individual and by it alone. Let's begin with the second point.

Capital is an exchange value (or, if you will, money) which grows; it is the self-growth of value. The problem is to know if capital grows on its own, in virtue of its own power—if money can make money—or if instead only the living individual has the power to make money and if it can only do this through the use of its own force, its "subjective labor force." In this latter case, the increase of value, the self-valorization of capital, is only apparent. It actually refers back to the action of the living individual and results exclusively from it. Capital is produced by the living force of the individual, by the "worker." Marx's brilliant proof of this will turn out to be a critique of capitalism as well as of the socialist regimes opposed to it.

In the circulation of goods on the market, that is to say in the exchange of goods, no increase of value can be introduced. Exchange is conditioned by the equality of the value of the exchanged goods: in principle, one exchanges goods of equal value. Where then does the increase of values come from, if not from the circulation of them?

On the marketplace, there must exist an extraordinary good that is no longer affected by any index of value (which would express the amount of labor needed for its production) and that has the important feature of being able to produce value on its own. This good is the living individual, who comes to sell him- or herself because he or she no longer has anything to offer besides his or her own force. In exchange for a certain amount of value or money (a wage), the capitalist purchases the use of this labor power, through which value will be produced. Let's recall that the production of value is only a representation or an exponent of real production, or, the actualization of the individual's living labor force. In the morning, this power of living labor will be used for the sake of producing a value that is equal to the wage; the employee "will reproduce" the value that has been invested by the capitalist. In the afternoon, this same force will produce a new value, equal to the one produced in the morning. This "produced" value is the added value. It expresses the surplus value created over the course of the day in relation to the value of the wage paid to the individual. Capital—the very possibility of capital, and, more generally, of every increase of value in the economy whatsoever—is based on this crucial phenomenon. What precisely does it consist of?

First, an essential displacement invites us to leave the superficial and loud world of the marketplace where values are exchanged in equal amounts and where they are actually believed to exist. This presupposition needs to be taken into account. To do this, we must go back to a "secret laboratory of production" in which values *are produced* before they are given in light of their objective measurement. Values are produced in the subjectivity of life where its force is deployed and where its living labor is carried out. Each value on the market results from the use of this force; the market value is only an objective representative of it. And, it is only possible for one value (the value of the wage) to give way to another value—for the reproduced value to give way to the surplus value—through a change of the level about which we are speaking. This occurs through the intervention of the labor power in the subjectivity where it is situated; its action alone creates the two new values. The growth of value and the appearance of new values are inexplicable on the economic level alone. This is why they imply the abandonment of it and a return to the original dimension where force produces the use object. Its value, at the same time, is only the index of this real production.

A question still remains: Why is the value of the wage less than the value that will be produced through labor power, in order for this gap to make surplus value possible, and thus to make the increased value of capital and even capital itself possible? The answer, once again, calls for us to leave the economic level and to go back to the level where life is infused in the individual and invests it with its force. The wage represents the value of things that are necessary for the maintenance of one's life, as we say, over the course of a day. This value—converted into food and other consumer goods—comes from the world of production; it is consumed by the worker and then disappears. In its place, what enters into play on the level of real production is the force of the labor purchased by the capitalist. Why does its use over the course of the day produce a value that is greater than the wage?

The value of the wage shows the amount of labor necessary for the production of the use values consumed by the laborer over the workday. The created value is the value of all the use values produced by him or her over the day. *That the created value is higher than the value of the wage is revealed outside of the economic sphere; it is revealed in the sphere of life in the following way: over this timespan, the living individual is able to create more use value than he or she needs in order to survive.* Here we discover an absolute property of life: its ability to give more than has been given to it, to produce more than it consumes. This "more" reveals one of the decisive traits of life: its metaphysical condition. Life is a power of growth. Beyond the vague desire to go beyond itself and surpass itself, it always has the actual ability to do so in virtue of the greater force it always carries within itself.

This fundamental property of life is the basis of every possible society, human development, and economic system—the capitalist system as well as the socialist system. Although they depend on the same basis, these two systems seem to be delivered over to different and opposed fates (this is the appearance that prevails today, at least). Before seeing how this can be the case, it is important first to think through to the end the determinant role of the individual within the economy. In this way, it will become all the more evident and undeniable to see what happens if the individual renounces this role—that is to say, renounces itself—dismisses its own responsibility, and its own force. In the mirror of the economy, we can see what results from the involvement as well as from the abstention of the individual: either life or death. But here again we need to grasp the principle behind all these phenomena. It will thus be necessary to leave the level of economics, because it has only ever been composed of indices. In order to decode them, it will be necessary to return to this origin of life and to this force on which everything depends.

The mystery of surplus value—of increased value and capital—has not been adequately clarified if all that has been established is that it comes from the individual's excess labor (from one's labor in the second half of the day), or even if it has been shown, as we have done, that it presupposes the "reproduction" of the wage's value. Let's again borrow an example from Marx.[1] A capitalist has invested capital in the amount of $100 in a process of production, which can be broken down as follows: $50 for cotton, $40 for wages, and $10 for instruments. Let's suppose that the instruments are totally consumed in the process and that the labor power carries out a period of excess labor that is equal to the time of necessary labor (that is to say, the labor necessary for the reproduction of the value of the wage). In exchange for $40 of his wage, the labor power produces a total value of $80 at the end of the process. However, $100 had been put forward at the beginning of the process: is it sold here for $20 less? Beyond the reproduction of the wage's value and the production of surplus value, this points to a third problem that has not yet been discussed but needs to be addressed. This problem concerns the conservation of the value of the objective conditions of the process: the instruments and the raw materials. This problem is essential, and it will lead us to the limits of a metaphysics of life.

In order for the process in our example to realize its capitalist purpose and produce a surplus value, it is important for the value of the instruments and materials to be conserved—in order to have at the end of the process $80 + $50 + $10 = $140 instead of the $100 initially invested. Although this is a mere conservation of value (the objective conditions of the process), it has nothing to do with the conservation of the commodities in the exchange. To be sure, when one exchanges $40 worth of tea for $40 and then for $40 worth of coffee, the value that the exchanger has in hand "remains"; it is identical throughout its three successive forms. But here one is considering the value of the commodity at the very moment that it is being exchanged. There is no need to wait: the tea could mold, the coffee could go stale, and the money could be devalued. The value of the exchanged goods keeps a determinant relation to their use value. After merchandise is degraded, its exchange value decreases as well. *The value of the exchanged goods at the moment of the exchange thus presupposes the conservation of their use value before the exchange.* The tautological identity of $40 of tea, $40, and $40 of coffee at the time of the exchange is a purely ideal identity that expresses the theoretical condition for this exchange. But it has no relation to the real conservation of the tea and coffee's exchange value; this presupposes the conservation of their use value. This real conservation of their use values is required in the real process of production, if it is to result in a surplus value. The exchange value of the cotton and tools—$50 + $10—must reappear at the end of the process in order to give it an overall value of $140.

Here Marx's analysis rejoins its decisive intuition: like the production of value, the simple conservation of value also takes place outside of the economic sphere, in the sphere of life and of living labor. The exchange value of goods can only be conserved, as we have said, if their use value is preserved. This condition is evident for all manufactured products that require maintenance and care; they would be irremediably lost without it. Although this fact may seem trivial, here a general metaphysical law is already revealed to us, namely, that things do not exist or subsist on their own, but only through a mysterious contact with life. It is only to the extent that life holds them in its grasp and keeps them in existence that they are able to escape from nothingness and death. Contrary to our ancestral beliefs, being does not actually reside in the thing or the object that is encountered by our regard and that seems to be self-sufficient—like the stones or rocks of mountains, like the earth of the plains, like the air in the sky or the water in rivers—they seem to exist on their own, in themselves, independently from and prior to human beings. But, anything that is seen, heard, smelled, or touched is only the correlate of an act of seeing, hearing, smelling, or touching. It would be nothing without these acts, that is, without the powers and forces that belong to our living body and to life. This is why nothing can exist in the world without life. Life is the alpha and the omega of the sensible as well as the intelligible world: of everything that is given to be experienced, to be understood, to be willed or to be loved. Everything that exists only has its being in life.

It is in the domain of the economy that this metaphysical truth can be recognized in its most immediate way. If we open our eyes to the world around us, we can see the mark of living labor everywhere within it. We can only see its results. Or, put better, we can only see its correlate—what it produces and continues to produce—because this labor does not end and cannot be interrupted at any single instant. The world is only the effect of praxis. The relation to the world through which the world is transformed is a practical relation. That is to say that it does not exist outside of this relation and comes to be what it is through it: its substance is living labor, the living individual himself. And this has been true as long as the Earth and human beings have existed. For the earth is itself only the ground on which we put our feet; it is the term that resists our efforts. This situation prevailed on the first day as much as it does today and as much as it did in the nineteenth century when Marx wrote: "And so it happens that in Manchester, for instance, Feuerbach only sees factories and machines, where a hundred years ago only spinning-wheels and weaving-looms were to be seen, or in the Campagna di Roma he finds only pasture lands and swamps, where in the time of Augustus he would have found nothing but the vineyards and villas of Roman capitalists."[2] But if the active force of life is deployed at the core of being, and if it is, rigorously speaking, an operation that makes being—an ontological operation—then the real process of production is only a particular case or better an exemplar of the operation that gives being. The economic process provides a figurative representation of this real process and is only intelligible on the basis of it.

Let's speak again about this economic process. It is now a question of understanding how the exchange values of tools and raw materials are conserved in this process so that they can reappear at its end. By being added to the reproduced value (the wage) and the produced value (the surplus value), they allow for the overall increase of value that capitalism presupposes. What is quite remarkable is that the tools and raw materials disappear from the real process of the production of exchange values: nothing enters into it other than the use values that correspond with it. To the extent that these use values are conserved, necessarily in a modified form, by the power of living labor that labors on them, so too the amount of labor included in them, that is to say, their exchange value, is conserved. This is why the analysis of the entire economic process and of each one of its elements—here the conservation of the value of its objective elements (raw materials and the instruments of labor)—requires us to return always to the single and omnipresent power of life that does everything in the real process. Life explains all of the avatars of the exchange value on the economic level.

How is the force of life conserved in modifying the raw materials that it labors on and the instruments through which it is able to do this? This crucial question is no different from the question of the ontological operation of life. We suggested that it underlies the human relation to the world and that "the transformation of nature by humans" is only its profane name. Through a set of concepts borrowed from Aristotle, Marx tried to explain how life's hold over things keeps them from nothingness. This hold is living labor; it is the necessarily singular and individual actualization of the force of life in a living body. Each act of living labor impresses a specific form on matter; matter would not exist without it. This form confers existence by making it into a particular material substance. The form impressed on matter by living labor is what Marx calls "objectified labor." In some sense, this is the structure of a thing that results from the hold of life. In being held by life and being structured by this hold, material substance conforms to life's hold in a foundational sense; it is ready for the "use" that life can or wants to make of it. It is in this original and decisive sense that it is a "use value."

But here is what is important. The form that living labor impresses on matter does not exist on its own, in virtue of its objective form or the matter that it informs. This means that the use value of the form that is impressed in the matter is not conserved through its own forces—it does not possess them. Left on its own, it would be destined to decay and ultimately to purely and simply disappear. Put otherwise, objectified labor in itself is dead labor. Here the metaphysics of life is revealed in its full reductive power: being can only exist as life and thus only in life. When separated from the force that maintains its being, every thing is destined for nothingness and returns to it without fail. This dialectic between dead labor and living labor finds its concrete expression in the fate of use values.

They are things-for-life not only in the sense that they have only been created for the sake of life, that is, for the use that life makes of them but also, and most importantly, in the sense that they can only exist in relation to this hold of life that has given form to them. They can exist only insofar as this hold remains. *Living labor is the ontological operation by which life sustains itself and experiences itself but at the same time sustains everything else that exists.* By contrast, when living labor is interrupted or ceases, then being collapses into nothingness. After no longer being held or used, a tool becomes deformed and unusable: the iron rusts, the port fills with sand, the barge rots and slowly sinks into the canal that stagnates, the channels or aqueducts break, the water spreads out into the fields that were fertile and transforms them into pestilent marshes. Raw materials, foodstuffs, and all other kinds of goods undergo the same fate: they are corrupted, rot, lose their usefulness, and disappear. In miserable marketplaces, lines of people form in front of empty stalls.

When living labor is understood as the sole source of all real and economic wealth, as the action that produces use values as well as the exchange values which are only the quantified representations of this action, then two case studies are offered. These depend on whether the force of life invested in living labor is developed to its greatest extent or whether, dissatisfied with itself and the world, it renounces its free and full exercise by placing itself on the dangerous road of refusing effort and by being content to do the least amount possible and even in some situations to no longer do anything at all. One is seriously mistaken, if one only sees these as isolated historical or local incidents, with limited and short-term effects. When it is a metaphysical force that supports everything that is weakened or interrupted, then this ontological deficit can neither be circumscribed nor limited. It involves everything: all of the use values and exchange values tumble downward. There is no longer any money to buy anything—or the money is no longer worth anything—but there is nothing there to be bought, either. In dismal boutiques, shoddy packages, and scarce but mediocre products all of a sudden acquire tremendous value. It is neither their use value nor their exchange value but some sort of mythical, imaginary, oneiric being. It is a sort of mirage that only exists to be situated at the limit of the possible and to represent the inaccessible term of desire.

In being separated from living labor, the world of tools has also lost all conceivable sense and purpose. Broken machines have had everything possible taken from them, stripped of their engines, closed workshops, deserted hangars with broken windows, depots closed for months or years, trolleys reaching up toward the sky that no human being will take hold of— these are not mere things, existing like rocks or earth. They are inhabited by a colossal lack that gnaws away at their dead presence, and indeed death has seized hold of this world where life, all of a sudden is no longer wanted. Life ceased to communicate the miracle of its force and its joy to this world. This is the world resulting from socialism. It has a funereal quality that gives it a family resemblance with fascism.

The second case study is capitalism. Here, without hesitation, one addresses life and the power of living labor.

6 LIFE AND DEATH IN THE CAPITALIST REGIME

Capitalism was not mistaken. It put its finger on what matters, on the only force that exists in the world which is the force of life, the force of living labor. Its instinctive behavior as well as its conscious decision was to base itself on living labor power. It put this force to work, established it as the condition for giving all that it can give, for accomplishing all that it can accomplish, and for "exploiting" it all the way. It carried out a project that was based on the hidden essence of reality, on the living force that produces everything and that, prior to even giving them "form," has the power to make things exist. For this ultimate reason—which is both metaphysical and ontological—capitalism gave rise to a revolution. It was the greatest revolution known throughout human history, or, to put it better, the only one.

For, a political revolution always runs along the surface of things or is merely a simulacrum like the democratization that is underway in the Eastern countries. An economic revolution can only be partial. It lets one particular layer remain unchanged, namely, economic reality itself. Capitalism, however, was a total revolution because it did not try to change anything about this sphere of the economy. Instead, capitalism understood that the economy was based on a deeper foundation, and so it deliberately turned toward it and addressed the one power that produces everything. It came to establish its reign by exalting this foundation and by bringing it to its culmination. This is how humanity has come to witness deeper changes over the last few decades, for better or worse, than over the previous millennia that go back to the obscure origins of humanity.

It was an opportunity as well as a risk for the nascent capitalism to find this force of living labor available. In the usual state of affairs, the force of life is not available. This is because the world is not separated from it, because the world is a lifeworld which only exists in and for life. It is the correlate of the powers of one's subjective corporeity. The world is what resists one's effort, and it only exists in this way, as this continual resistance from the Earth. Life, in turn, cannot be disconnected from what constantly holds it in its grasp: from the air that it breathes, from the ground that it treads, from the tool that it uses, or from the object that it sees. The original co-belonging of the living individual and the Earth is essentially practical. It is located in life and based on it. The force of life is the force through which the Individual and the Earth cohere in this ageless origin (*primitivité sans âge*). Living labor is the implementation of this force. It is not an accidental event occurring on the surface of the Earth and affecting the individual from the outside, instead it is the actualization from within of the power through which life holds the universe. Held in this power, things are from the outset what they are shown to be through the action of living labor: they are materials to be informed by its living force, the tools of this force, its ready-made "extensions," and informed by it. Inasmuch as they are held by life and life maintains them in being, raw materials, and tools are the correlate and extension of life. They belong to it in principle. It is in this way that the human is the proprietor of the Earth. The human is situated in this primal co-belonging of the Universe and Life.

To make labor power available, it was necessary to break this primal co-belonging and co-ownership. Life adheres to raw materials and tools with all its being, but they were taken away from life. This ontological rupture was disguised as a historical event. This occurred through the seizing (*accaparement*) of communal goods by large landowners, the expropriation of peasants, and their arrival on the marketplace as "free" workers. This means that after being stripped of all the means of production, they are reduced solely to their labor power. This, at least, remained in place, as their only potential force in their precarious and overwhelming life. The genius of the capitalist was to perceive this force for what it was—and to buy it.

Marx's genius was to perceive that, unlike an ordinary purchase, this exchange of capital for labor was not an exchange. And that is why every "market" economy is vicious (*viciée*) in principle. An exchange always occurs between two identical exchange values: $40 of tea for $40 or for $40 of coffee. The capital/labor exchange is not vicious merely because it takes place between two quantitatively unequal exchange values. It is vicious *because it does not take place between two exchange values at all; what faces the exchange value put forward by the capitalist—the value of the salary—is a use value.* What is hired is truly the fundamental use value; namely, the use of the worker's living labor power. *In exchange for a given and calculated value, the capitalist does not obtain another value but the creative force of value: living labor power.* Afterwards, the fate of capitalism is set. Since all capital seeks to valorize itself and since it is only a certain amount of value or money that seeks to increase again and again, it then becomes a question of implementing this labor power more and more. For it alone has the power to produce this value that needs to grow and to produce more than it costs—that is, more than the amount of labor inscribed in the subsistence that it needs in order to be maintained.

It is already known how capitalism assumed its fate of being a value in search of valorization: by exploiting the force of life. It made men, women, and children work 10 to 15 hours per day, and it made them do so at an unbridled pace, without breaks, without any regard for their pain, fatigue, rest, shelter, education, or dignity. In short, it had no regard for the daily lives of the workers from whom it only sought to obtain their force, all their force. It was by sucking up this force and feeding itself from it—by sucking the blood of living labor like a vampire, to repeat a recurrent expression in Marx's texts—that the valorization of capital and thus capital itself were possible. The production of use values only happens in the "melting pot of production," where living labor restrains, disfigures, burns, bends under its flame, disintegrates, and liquefies raw materials in order to rebuild, restructure, re-organize, re-shape, and "reawaken them from the dead." In short, these materials acquire a new configuration that will turn them into use values. Likewise, as a result of the burning fire of living labor that creates use values, their exchange value is produced at the same time as them. It, too, results from this burning kiss of life; it depends on this and exposes its marks—it is nothing but their objective representation.

We have shown that the economic world as a whole is an objective representation of living labor and that it is composed of entities that are its substitutes, its quantifiable equivalents. Henceforth, the meaning of the economic components of the process turns out to be twofold: positive and negative at the same time. To the extent that the exchange value exposes the amount of labor included in goods, it refers to living labor, through the social and abstract labor that leads to this quantification. The exchange value exhibits it precisely and lets it be seen; it allows it to be counted. As an indication of living labor, exchange value is a direct expression that sticks to it in some sense, and it is only possible by being engendered at each moment by living labor. The exchange value is unequivocally the true motor of the economic system. Every economic constituent and every value is the result and at the same time the representative of this force.

One cannot forget, however, its nature—its objective, ideal, and abstract character. Just as the irreal is opposed to the real, it is opposed to the living labor for which it is the indication. An irreal representation, such as an imaginary one, can still be adequate to the reality to which it responds. In his photo, it is indeed Pierre himself who one sees "in an image" for a second time, so to speak. *This is not the case for living labor in its relation to abstract or social labor.* The inadequation introduced between them is not due solely to the difference that divides the real from the irreal. The singular properties of the real labor of a specific individual—the intensity of one's effort, the pain, the boredom, or satisfaction that is experienced during its completion—cannot be found at all, even in an irreal form, in the social labor that the economist substitutes for them. Instead, the economist abstracts from the characteristics that vary with each individual in terms of one's individual capacities or talents. What is retained is a norm, the idea of a certain type of labor, instead of the various ways in which it is actually experienced. Labor defined socially—as lifting a weight or building a wall—is only the same on the level of this objective definition. But, for the worker who performs it, it is different each time. This difference hollows out an abyss into which all of the equivalencies by which economic reality is defined fall. And along with this system of equivalencies and their supposed adequation, so too does all order and social justice.

Here we encounter the economic or rather the meta-economic foundation of the aporia of social justice. In chapter 3, we showed how this aporia corrupts every regime that claims to be built on this impossible justice, especially the communist regimes. What is just is to give the same salary for the same labor. But the same objective labor is altogether different from its real subjective actualization. To give the same salary for various labors that are really different, that is injustice itself. "This equal right," as Marx says abruptly in his "Critique of the Gotha Program," "is an unequal right for unequal labor."[1] This is why a deep malaise comes to permeate the economic world and, through its introduction, the entire human world. The tribunal where one delivers social justice ought to reveal their merits, their real effort, and their talents, but in fact it is the site of a permanent perversion that is so complete that it escapes from any well-founded assessments. In order to overcome the impossibility of measuring the pain and effort of each individual, the economic system of substitutions was invented. But this system is broken by this impossibility.

The shadow that looms over the human city is due to the impossibility of measuring the merit of each individual. It darkens even more when one notices that it is precisely under the cover of this shadow that the crucial phenomenon in the production of surplus value—exploitation—is hidden. Here the defect of the capitalist regime can be added to the defect of the market economy which always substitutes objective equivalents for life. The capitalist regime refers to and presupposes the market economy. *It is precisely because the objective equivalent—in this case the wage—is unable to demonstrate its equivalence to real labor, that it is able to pay the same wage for different labor.* For example, it is able to pay the wage for a whole day in place of the wage for a half day. Is not the former wage twice the latter? This is only the case for objective equivalents—like the objective duration of real labor —but it is not the case for their subjective reality: the intensity of effort and its efficacy. Any measure is arbitrary and contingent here. It is thanks to this contingency that capitalist exploitation and the malaise of the worker are able to develop.

But here is something more severe. Up to now, we have always taken the real process of production as a point of departure, and we have understood the economic process as a translation of it into a system of numerical equivalents. However contestable this equivalence might be, economic determinations—values of merchandise, wages, etc.—have always had the character of "representing" living labor. The real process is the origin, while the economic process is the effect: the former is the principle, while the latter is the result. Or rather, the former is precisely the real process, while the latter is only a copy of it. The capitalist regime reverses this fundamental relation. It carries out a true ontological subversion at the end of which it is the result, the product—value or capital—that is taken as the motor of the whole system. By contrast, the force that produces all of the economic determinations is integrated into them. It only appears as one determination among others, under the imprecise name of "labor."

This subversion can be recognized on the level of exchange, whose original vital signification actually gets reversed. In traditional economics, exchange is only a means for each participant in exchange to obtain what he or she needs in return for the object that is given: exchange is only motivated by the use value of products. The exchange value has no other aim than to make it possible. With the money coming from the sale of a commodity that one no longer needs, it is possible to procure another commodity which one lacks, according to the CMC formula "commodity—money—commodity." The capitalist only buys commodities with the aim of obtaining through its sale a higher amount than what it was purchased for. Commodities are exchanged, as we have seen, for an equal value, so this is only possible if the capitalist has the good luck to find on the marketplace an extraordinary commodity that has the power to produce value.

But what matters to us here is the simple inversion of the purpose of the exchange: it is no longer the use value but money. The formula of exchange is then MCM (money–commodity–money). The amount of money at the end of the process of exchange must be greater than the initial amount. This is the formula of valorization and of capital. It shows that henceforth it is an economic reality—money—that becomes the sole aim of production. This inversion of the original vital purpose of exchange signifies the inversion of the relation between the two processes of production: real and economic. Up to then, the latter was only a means that enabled the real production to be carried out, for life to gain hold of the commodities that it created to be used. Afterwards, it is the contrary: the process of life becomes nothing more than a way of producing money.

When life processes are subjected to economic processes, their internal structure is profoundly changed. As long as production seeks the satisfaction of human needs, it is limited like them. It is held within the closed circle of possibilities that define each phase of human history. But the production of money is unlimited. Money is a pure quantity to which a new quantity can always be added. The aim of capitalism is to add a new quantity to the already existing quantity of money. Dismissed of its own vital ends, real processes become nothing but the servants of the continual production of money. Before examining the transformations occurring to the internal structure of real processes due to the exclusive search for money, it is important to evaluate the full magnitude of this inversion of the relation between these two processes of production: real and economic.

It means, first of all, that the play is henceforth performed by the understudies. The substitute elements in the economic process will come to play the role of the true causes in the real process. This is a paradoxical situation: the real element, living labor, is subjected to its irreal double; that is, to the ideal identity whose role was to allow for a measurement of reality. Value can and should only signal the intervention of life—its punctual and permanent action—after the fact; however, value becomes its only reason. And if production and the growth of value are no longer desirable or simply are no longer possible, then it is life—the movement of desire toward its satisfaction—that no longer has any reason to exist! On the one hand, the economic process is merely a reflection that represents real labor, but, on the other hand, it is the sole reason for its implementation; that is to say, for the possibility of life to continue to live. This confers a sort of madness on the economic process, in principle. This madness consists of a reflection, an appearance, that has become the sole principle for action.

In order to analyze this placement of the economic process over the vital process and its claim to replace it, we need to proceed in two directions. First, it needs to be shown that this substitution is illusory. The economic process is indeed composed of replacement parts—all the ideal entities that correspond to the real constituents of the vital process. But these entities are only abstractions. As mere representatives of living labor power, they cannot take its place or bring about any sort of action. They can neither produce use values nor exchange values; they can only represent this real production that occurs through the subjective force of life. As an extension of his critique of the market economy, Marx's critique of capitalism is based on this decisive idea that economic reality is only a substitute reality and, moreover, an abstraction. This critique thus has an overwhelming intelligibility that makes it invincible. *No abstraction or ideality has ever been able to produce a real action; consequently, it can only represent it. No value is able to grow on its own, nor can it reproduce itself or conserve itself.* The principle behind capital, which would be a value of this kind, is thus unmasked.

What is said about exchange value also holds for the entirety of economic reality. Economic reality is actually only a modified form of value and only a phase of its development. It is only one of the multiple ways that value can appear in a world that is only made up of its successive appearances, declensions, and "metamorphoses." It is an important sign of progress to understand the economic world in its homogeneity—that is to say, in all of its determinations—and to understand that they are all values in the economic sense, in the sense of exchange value. To the extent that one has understood living labor as the principal and unique source of exchange value, then one also has grasped the principle and source of all economic determinations. They are the forms in which this value appears. Profit, for example, signifies a growth of value; its substance is surplus value. Like the production of surplus value, the production of profit takes place on the level of life and of living labor. Its intelligibility requires one to leave the economic level in order to understand what, in the sphere of life, allows it to produce more use value than it consumes and thus to produce more exchange value than it costs. Everything having to do with profit, its modes of calculation—profit rates and interests rates—or its modes of distribution—interest financing, property rental, etc.—implies the prior existence of surplus value. Surplus value, in turn, is only comprehensible on the basis of profit: its modes of calculation, being shared out, etc. Yet, first of all, it is only intelligible on the basis of its source: living labor and excess labor.

All forms of capital are forms of value. They lend themselves to increasingly complex analyses by starting first from elementary distinctions like those between productive, commercial, and financial capital. Productive capital itself can be described variously in which it appears as "fixed capital" or "circulating," or even as "variable capital" or "constant." Each of these conceptual forms of capital—that is to say of economic value—can be translated in turn within mathematical parameters. On this basis, one can then construct increasingly sophisticated mathematical models. As is known, the modern economy grants this mathematization of economic reality an increasingly large importance.

The true problem is the problem concerning the sense of these analyses as well as of the various conceptual systems within which they are formulated. Are they limited to economic reality *stricto sensu*, that is, to the forms of value? In this case, the proper morphology of economic phenomena are demonstrated by presupposing that this description will have an explanatory value. Or rather: economic phenomena are explained economically. Marx's insight was to denounce this illusion and to treat all economic phenomena as mere appearances. Instead of providing a principle of explanation, they have to be explained. When economic phenomena are conceptualized on the basis of their economic appearance, one is dealing with concepts like productive, commercial, or financial capital, fixed or circulating capital, variable or constant capital. But, among these concepts, which ones should be privileged and provide the premises that explain the analysis?

One cannot understand economic phenomena by remaining on the level of the economic phenomena themselves, their morphology and the concepts that express them. Economically, the concepts of productive, commercial, and financial capital have an equal status. It is just as legitimate to contrast fixed capital and circulating capital as to form another pair: variable capital and constant capital. These morphological analyses are only actually a description of their current values and their history. They do not in any way explain the formation of such values, and they are silent about their genesis, that is to say, the power that produces them and that lets them exist and grow. The parameters explaining the size of these existing values and their evolution only translate a state of affairs that they presuppose instead of explain.

To account for the world of values—that is to say all of the economic determinations—is thus to be situated outside of this world. It is to return to the power that produces values. The vicissitudes that affect values and the economic parameters are only ever indicated after the fact. They necessarily refer to the vicissitudes of labor power and to the history of life itself. Even more deeply still, they refer to the essence of life, to its internal conditions and to its ability to surpass its needs. This is the first direction of an authentic economic analysis. Its radical sense is to go back to a meta- or extra-economic aspect of the economy that can explain it. And, it also explains capitalism; namely, the process of the growth of value that is made possible by appealing to the power that produces this value and its growth at each moment, and by the use of this power. The meta-economic, or better infra-economic, analysis of capitalism shows how life can be found everywhere, as the basis of capitalism and as the principle that ensures its triumph.

Death can also be found there, and this is how. The substitution of the real process of production by representatives or objective, ideal equivalents that are able to measure them and thus allow for the exchange of products is not innocent. Truly speaking, it is not a mere substitution at all, as is still the case in the market economy. With capitalism, as we have seen, the purpose of exchange and of the whole economic process has been reversed. It no longer concerns the production of the use values that are needed to satisfy the participants in exchange; instead it is about the production of money. This new purpose of the economic process will react against the vital process and overturn its internal structure. The economic process then turns out to no longer be a mere copy of the real process; it is not a copy that simply repeats its movements, like the shadow of a traveler on the road. The production of exchange value in the economic process is based on the production of use values in the real process and is only possible through it. But, the new purpose assigned by capitalism to the economic process—the continual obligation to produce more money—can only be realized if, in the real process, the conditions for this unlimited production of money are put in place and themselves realized.

To produce more money is to produce more surplus value. There are two ways to increase the production of surplus value. In the first place, one can increase the time of excess labor at the expense of the time of necessary labor, such that the time over the day that the worker devotes to the production of surplus value is increased in relation to the time needed for the reproduction of the value of the wage, that is to say, the production of the goods needed in order to maintain one's ability to work. This can be done by extending the workday, as was the case in the nineteenth century. But this extension has its limits, whereas the production of surplus value or money must not have any limits. So, the second way is to develop the productivity of real labor. By making the labor necessary for maintaining the worker increasingly shorter, this frees up a time for longer excess labor, even though the length of the day remains the same.

With the development of productivity within the real process, we are brought to the core of the history of capitalism which is also the history of the world. This history is not a history of events (*histoire evenementielle*); it is not a series of accidents that could only be recounted afterwards. It is a history of principles (*histoire principielle*), based not on an ordinary set of facts but on what should be called original facts or "Archi-facts"—it is based on a supra-temporal power that is always present and active. It is situated in history and yet is meta-historical; it precedes it in a way and determines it *a priori*. To the extent that it obeys an ever-present power within itself, history does not move forward by chance. It obeys a tendency that translates this continual action of the same principle into history. Capitalism exposes this action in full clarity and allows it to be recognized, if one were to pierce the veil of economic phenomena that result from it at the same time as they hide it. In capitalism more than any other regime, one can discern the "tendency" of history and understand why it is a history of tendencies (*histoire tendancielle*).

This tendency has a strange and even terrible meaning. It is rooted in life. In this sense, it is the tendency of life itself, which is ultimately guided by the will to live. Moreover, we already know that an ever present and active principle orients history at each moment and that this principle is none other than and can be none other than life. Life is the only force and the only reality. It is the continual reiteration of need and desire. Need and desire arouse the continual repetition of the "actions" that aim to satisfy them.

But, in capitalism, the teleology of life aiming to satisfy its desires is inverted. It affects the internal structure of the real process of production through the continual development of productivity. Is this simply a "technical" modification of the real process? With this modification, however, the history of capitalism connects with the history of the world and illuminates it in a tragic light. The tendency that resides in history turns into its opposite and becomes the tendency of death.

7 THE EMPIRE OF DEATH: THE TECHNOLOGICAL-ECONOMIC WORLD

It is only possible to decrease the time of necessary labor in order to increase the role of surplus labor and thus of surplus value through an increase of the productivity of labor. This seemingly economic law only becomes evident if it is related to the real process of production of use values that are its foundation. Here, outside of the economy, we are nothing but life. Life is alone with itself and the world, which "belongs" to it as the correlate of its praxis, as a lifeworld. In an archaic "economy" which does not yet have an economic reality in the proper sense, it is first a question of the survival of life. That is to say that one acquires subsistence goods each day, and, more generally, the objects that life urgently needs in order not to die—from hunger, cold, or all kinds of aggressions. This is the original situation. It is pure in the sense that it is a limit situation at the same time as it reveals the ultimate condition of life. This condition is expressed in a relation between what life needs and what it is able to produce. The fact that this relation defines the condition of life results from the fact that the inability to produce what is absolutely necessary would immediately signify death. This figure has been encountered more than once in history, even if no historian was there to record the dramatic turns of events.

Conversely, when the capacity to produce necessary goods increases even a little bit, it is clear that life can untie the yoke of necessity that has restrained and determined all of its behavior from the beginning. How does this capacity to produce come to be increased? It occurs due to the production of tools that render the acquisition of indispensable goods less precarious. This is how a gap opens up between "what life needs" and "what it is able to produce." Everything that we call by the name of civilization and culture comes to be established in this gap.

It is thus not unimportant to note that the possibility of this gap—through producing more than is needed—is the possibility of life in the sense of its ownmost power. The ability to live is based on this absolutely positive power. Is this power only the expression of a contingent fact? Is it only the expression of the fact that an empirical individual has the ability to create more useful things than he or she consumes? Or is it based on the innermost essence of life, on its pathos? Is it based on the fact that each of the individual's powers—and first each of the individual's needs—coheres with the self with a force that flows back into them, immerses them and exalts them by giving this need the force to complete itself—"power" is just another name for this force—the power to surpass itself?

The ability of life to produce more than it needs is so deeply buried in the self that we have ceased to perceive it under the accumulation of sediment that covers it over, and especially under the edifice of economic phenomena that have copied the "real process," that is ultimately to say, this power of life. And the more this economic world unfolds with its increasingly sophisticated system of equivalents—with its parameters and mathematical models—the more obscure the source from which they proceed becomes. The economic sciences have never known a more sophisticated development, but they have never known less about what they are seeking or what they are talking about.

In the real, hidden process that underlies the entire economic world, the problem is now to identify with greater precision how the growth of productivity—which is required by the continual growth of surplus value—modifies the internal constitution of production to the point of entirely subverting it. The more productive one's labor becomes, the sooner the worker will have reproduced the value of the wage and the sooner the worker will be devoted exclusively to the production of surplus value. The sooner, in other words, one's labor power will be offered to capitalist exploitation. Since the length of the workday is fixed or even decreased, it is thus productivity alone that will determine whether the surplus value is merely maintained or grows.

It is necessary to define productivity in a rigorous way. This concept seems to be self-evident, but it can be shown to be completely ambivalent. It is only by dispelling this ambivalence that one can recognize in the world around us—the world we are calling techno-capitalist—the feature by which it oddly resembles the socialist regimes that are on the verge of collapsing. It happens to be like them in eliminating the living individual, and in spite of the overly obvious differences between them, it turns out to be threatened by death.

Productivity, at first, does not mean anything besides the efficiency of production, its aptitude to create useful products quickly and well— products that are useful for life. We have identified the creative capacity of this production with living labor, that is to say with the activity of life itself, and, even more profoundly, with the force that makes use of this activity. This creative force of living labor is production considered in terms of its subjectivity. Production, as we have said, also has objective elements: the tools of labor and raw materials. How and why these objective elements belong to the subjective force of living labor is what we have sought to understand on the basis of the original co-belonging of life and the world. In other words, by recusing every external description, we must re-establish ourselves within subjective activity and experience the world only as the correlate of its power, the term that resists or gives way to its effort. Through its resistance or giving way, the world is originally given to the subjective force of life as its "tool" or its "material."

If increased productivity is understood as the efficiency of subjective production, this can only mean an increase in the efficiency of the force of life. In the end, it is to lead it to be delivered entirely in the same time as fully drawing an advantage from one's skill, in this repeated exercise. To increase this efficiency is to increase the power of this force. The tools invented over the course of human history have permitted this little by little, although this growth was necessarily finite. For tools are informed by labor power that handles and controls them; they are held in its grasp. By bending to and receiving their structure from the force of labor, tools also received their force from it. This force is increased by the use of a lever, or extended further by sticks, poles or clubs, but it still remains an extension of a very limited power, namely, the power of the individual. This is why, as long as the augmentation of surplus value had to be conferred by the intensification of this subjective force, it remained weak like this force. The only means for the capitalist—for the capitalist before capitalism—was to exploit this force as much as possible and to extend the workday up to the brink of exhaustion. In China, the coolies carried overly heavy loads along unending paths until they collapsed on the road in front of the indifferent eyes of those who, stepping over their bodies, continued along their path. But the production of surplus value—production in general—remained as lethargic as those who are numbed by opium.

The systematic and unremitting exploitation of labor power with the aim of satisfying the economic process of the production of money would not have been able to fulfill its own purpose nor would the real process of the production of use values have been able to increase its powers in such dramatic fashion, unless an extraordinary event that is too quickly attributed to capitalism had not occurred along with it and allowed for its rise. This event marks the true turning point in the history of humanity and the beginning of modernity, but it was covered over and hidden by the great economic development that it made possible. This is the development of surplus value. And since the production of surplus values involves surplus labor, it was freed in new proportions and new conditions.

This event is not a mere fact but an Archi-fact. This is a decisive transformation of something that, though situated in history, is neither swept away nor abolished by history; instead, it remains present at each point of its journey, in such a way as to be its guiding principle. We are already familiar with an Archi-fact of this kind: it is life. Life is historical because it seems to be born and to die with each individual in history; however, it is meta-historical to the extent that it is life. In life, there is the continual reiteration of need and labor. At each instant of this history, it makes history be what it is, namely, a history of production and consumption.

Unlike life, the second meta-historical fact does not create history, instead it imposes a definite direction on history after it has occurred. This is the Galilean Archi-fact. Its historical expression consists of the fact that the real process of production henceforth ceases to be subjective and identified with living labor. To be sure, however archaic it may be, the real process of production necessarily involves objective elements: tools and raw materials. But, production in itself—action—was subjective; it consisted of the inner deployment of the subjective force of the living body. Moreover, tools and raw materials were only the extensions—the points of application or of resistance—of this force. They were known and handled by this force. Truly speaking, it could only be said that they were known through this subjective handling of them, such that the knowledge at work in the production of useful goods was this force itself. More profoundly, this was the subjectivity through which one comes to know oneself. It is precisely to the extent that force is experienced immediately in its absolute subjectivity that it enters into possession of itself and that it is able to be deployed and to act.

With Galileo, to the contrary, the encounter with the world is stripped of its essential subjectivity. The task of understanding the world in its true being is no longer assigned to bodily sensible knowledge nor to the subjective force that inhabits the body. The world is no longer made up of sensible qualities that are grasped through subjective powers, instead it is made up of material, extended bodies that are delineated by their shape. As a result, the only rigorous, adequate, and rational knowledge of the world that we can acquire is the ideal knowledge of the shapes of these bodies. It is geometrical knowledge. The world, according to Galileo's famous metaphor, is a great book that we are only able to read by knowing its language. Its letters are the "triangles, circles and other geometrical figures without which it is not humanly possible to understand its speech."[1]

Afterwards, Descartes was able to offer a mathematical formulation of this geometric knowledge of the world, and then modern science—the physical-mathematical approach to material being—was born.

This substitution of geometrical-mathematical knowledge of the material world for its bodily, subjective, and living apprehension entails a subversion of the phenomenon of action, which is located at the core of traditional production. This subversion is worthy of being called ontological, in the sense that *it is action in its very being that is changed; it is no longer subjective but objective.* Instead of being produced in the life of individuals and instead of putting into play the powers that they experience internally, this action—or what continues to be wrongly identified by this term—subsequently occurs before the regard of thought. It occurs as a set of objective processes that are analogous to natural processes. These natural processes—physical, electro-magnetic, chemical, biological, or others like them—will come to define the being of action, instead of and in place of the living, suffering, and acting subjectivity of human beings. This ontological displacement is also a phenomenological displacement. It is one and the same movement that produces the substitution of objective natural movements for the subjective action of living individuals and conjointly produces the substitution of objective and rational knowledge of the material world for an invisible and felt inner experience that life has of itself at every moment and that is its own subjectivity.

If "technology" is the name for the set of procedures involved in the transformation of nature by human beings for the sake of making it suitable to human needs, one sees that the concept of technology is even more equivocal than the concept of productivity with which it is identified. To remove this ambiguity, it is necessary to distinguish radically between traditional technology whose reign extends from the beginning of humanity up to the middle of the nineteenth century (to give it an approximate limit) and technology in the modern, Galilean sense. Technology cannot be limited simply to the set of instruments or tools that are used in a specific line of work. This would only seem to be the case in modern technology. As a form of know-how, technology also includes action. In traditional technology, action is revealed in its specificity. It is the implementation of the subjective force of life, and its tools are derived from this subjective force. They are only "extensions" of it. The knowledge at stake here is the knowledge of life, that is, of its pure subjectivity. In this knowledge, the living body is in possession of its powers and able to put them to use.

In modern technology, subjectivity disappears, or, rather, it is reduced to the physical-mathematical knowledge of the material world. "Tools" have taken over its place. They include a set of material devices that are increasingly complex, that are derived from nature, and that are objective like nature. They are constructed in light of the physical-mathematical knowledge introduced by Galileo. This is the reason why modern technology is situated immediately after science and tends to be confused with it. Moreover, it is modern technology, as a growing collection of machines and high-powered machines, that summons science to answer the problems posed by its own development. This development becomes autonomous and, as an auto-development, is the development of science and technology, or in other words, a techno-science. The legitimacy of this concept is thus complete.

Let's now project this radical change of technology onto what we have been calling from the beginning of our analyses "the real process of production." This process is identified with the full concept of technology. It is a transformation of nature by the human being as well as the set of procedures involved in this transformation. We then come across the central insight of Marx's thought: the subversion of the internal structure of "productive forces." These refer to nothing other than the real process of production, that is to say, to technology understood in an exhaustive sense. The transformation of the productive forces that will guide the fate of the modern world must then be formulated as follows: subjectivity—living labor—is progressively eliminated from the real process of production, whereas the role of objective instrumental devices continues to grow. Or instead: the process of labor and the process of production diverge. This is another way to express the decline of subjective labor power in a process that is increasingly devoted to objectivity.

It is necessary to assess this transformation and to see how it signifies a complete change of the world in which we live, because it entails a complete overturning of our own lives. In traditional "technology," life coincides with the activities through which it produces necessary goods—it is fully invested in these activities and is defined by them. Life is what it does in order to live and survive. Material production thus defines human existence, imposing its own rhythm as well as its "content" onto it. Modern technology, by contrast, is confined to instrumental objective devices that are increasingly automated, and its mode of production gradually but invincibly excludes the subjective activity of human beings—that is, their own existence. It remains and will continue to remain outside of the process of production. The rigid prescription of a certain number of acts disappears along with it. The force of life remains unemployed, just like the individual. It is not only the social phenomenon of unemployment that emerges as a necessary result of the transformation of productive forces;

it also signifies a new condition for life in which its energy and libido is unemployed: anxiety. For this, the world of technology immediately offers palliatives—television in developed countries, and vodka or some other narcotic in developing countries—or both at the same time. But we have other more urgent comments that need to be made.

Having shed light on the radical transformation of the "technology" of the real process of production, let's now shed light on the economic process. More precisely, we will see what this process becomes when, with the inversion of vital teleology, capitalism delivers it over to the production of money. Money is nothing but exchange value in its pure form. Let's recall the thesis that Marx borrowed directly from the English school and indirectly from the Bible. According to this thesis, all value comes from labor: "you will earn your bread through the sweat on your brow." Obviously, this claim gave rise to many critiques on the part of economists, especially modern economists. The inanity of their critiques is precisely due to the fact that, on Marx's view, *the presupposition that value originates in labor does not belong to the economic order.* It is not and cannot be because "labor" does not belong to the economic order, either.

It should not be forgotten that Marx's decisive critique of the English school—namely, of Smith and Ricardo—was that their concept of labor was indeterminate. Marx considered his great discovery to be the crucial distinction between real, subjective, and living labor, on the one hand, and social and abstract labor, on the other hand. It is only on this basis that the thesis that labor creates value can acquire its meaning. The labor in question is in fact living labor; it is the subjective force of life. Then, the foundation of value—the foundation of the entire economic world—becomes situated deliberately and explicitly outside of the economy. Under these conditions, the question is no longer to know what "determines" value, its fluctuations, and all of its avatars. Such a question refers back to the marketplace as the place and principle for this determination. This is a naïve answer. Instead of being able to explain anything at all, what happens on the marketplace is precisely what needs to be explained. Moreover, even when the conditions of the marketplace are understood as the true object of the analysis, these conditions remain economic ones. This is to posit, at least implicitly, that economic phenomena are derived from an economic interpretation.

But there is no value in nature, no more than there are circles or triangles in it. The existence of a dimension of pure ideality where geometric figures are constructed is the inescapable and tacit presupposition of geometry. This presupposition refers back to its "origin," that is, to the transcendental act of the mind which has created this dimension prior to the figures in it.

And, likewise, the fluctuations of value on the marketplace as well as their economic conditions outside of the market presuppose the existence of something like an exchange value. It does not exist on its own, like a thing. Instead, it too refers to a transcendental genesis. Without it, humans would never have had to do with value, with any economic value at all or with the economic world in general. This non-economic origin of the economy is life. Its force and its needs have an internal and hidden connection. They produce economic phenomena in a metaphysical sense before they are determined in the economic world where they will emerge at the same time as life.

After establishing the meta-economic meaning of the thesis that labor— in truth, the force of life—produces economic value along with the economy, after thus understanding the economic process of production in its genesis from life, the projection the modern essence of technology onto life illuminates it through and through like the flash of lighting that lights up the night. Let's recall the almost inconceivable subversion that modern technology brought about. The original appropriation of Life and the World is guided by the principle of life. Living labor is its actualization. It is subjectivity that does everything and that holds the world in its hands. The elimination of the subjectivity that holds this primitive relation together is the paradox that modern technology accomplishes little by little, to the extent that it replaces this hold on life with insensitive objective processes. This is how action leaves the domain of living subjectivity in order to be transformed into the indifferent phenomena of micro-physics. Projected onto the real process of production, identified with it and restructuring it from within, modern technology thus signifies the gradual diminution of living labor and the increasing role of objectivity in this process.

If living labor creates exchange value, then the projection of the essence of modern technology onto the economic process can be expressed as follows: *the gradual elimination of living labor from the real process of production signifies its increasing inability to produce value.* But the production of value is economic production as such; it is the economic process. *The transformation of the internal structure of the real process of production, as a result of modern technology, implies the underlying impossibility of the economic process.* What, in turn, does this impossibility of the economic process signify? What makes it impossible?

It makes impossible precisely what the economic process had made possible and that for which it had been invented. What should be remembered is the genesis of the economic process from the process of life. This should be done by considering the dual form of the economic process over the course of its history: first as a process of exchange in the market economy and then as a process of the production of money in the capitalist economy.

The economic process was invented in order to allow the exchange of products that were created by life to satisfy its needs. This leads to the invention of exchange value. By calculating the amount of labor involved in each product, this value allows it to be exchanged in terms of every other value on the same index. At this stage of its history, when its genesis is still transparent, the economic process allows the real process to be carried out. It allows the various use values resulting from production to be submitted to the division of labor and to pass from the hands of those who produce them into the hands of those who consume them.

The transparency of this genesis of exchange value does not prevent the opacity on which we have insisted at great length: the fact that each subjective modality of labor power is separated by an abyss from the quantifiable objective equivalent to which one seeks to make it correspond. In this enigmatic duplication of life by a series of abstract entities, these entities cannot fail to function in virtue of their proper nature, however abstract they may be. This abstraction is even what allows them to function. For example, the exchange value is purified of all matter and of everything that makes up the concrete reality of specific use values. For this reason, it can be tied to one or another of these use values indifferently. Whether one is determining $40 of coffee or $40 of tea, the $40 has nothing to do with the coffee or the tea. It is an ideal representation of the labor from which they result. In its ideal function, the exchange value seems to be autonomous, to follow its own trajectories, and to obey connections and regulations that are specifically economic—even if, by means of abstract labor, it refers to the reality of the living labor for which it is a mere example and even if, as the value of commodities, it refers also to a use value of commodities. Value thus continues to maintain an inescapable relationship with life, with its needs and with its labor. The economy copies life, but life produces the economy. It constantly returns the economy to itself, and it is in this deep sense that it can be said to "determine" the economy.

When the market economy becomes capitalist, its autonomy is affirmed resoundingly. The exchange value, which up to then was only a means, now becomes the purpose of the new process. Constituted henceforth as a process of development, it acts in return on the components of the real process. It requires the role of necessary labor to continue to decrease to the benefit of surplus labor. As powerful as the action in return by the process of development on the real process may be, it remains subordinate to the inverse determination and is overdetermined by it. For, it is living labor and it alone that can produce value and thus produce the increase of value that defines capitalism.

Here is where the crucial Event occurs. Yet, as long as it is conceived as the reaction of the economic process to the real process, it can only be defined superficially. This reaction is a modification of the internal structure of the real process with the subordination of necessary labor to surplus labor. As long as this subordination remains in place and regardless of its effects on the process of development as well as on the life of individuals, it is precisely this—living labor—that is in question. Our continual attention is on this decisive fact. Regardless of the frenetic pace that the economic process imposes on living labor, this process is produced and overdetermined by living labor throughout. Because the economic process is produced by the real process and because it is constantly based on it, it can only carry out its continual development by tearing this process away from living labor. Exploitation is the exploitation of living labor. It reconnects with our broad theme of the foundation of the economy in life. And in its extreme formulation, it reconnects with the image of the vampire, of capital sucking the blood out of living labor. But it is precisely no longer that.

The Event that demands our attention now—the Arrival of techno-capitalism—no longer maintains this major reference of capitalism to life. This reference was discovered by "exploitation": it eliminates this. The domination of surplus labor over necessary labor was required by the exclusive production of money, and it called for an important modification of the internal structure of the real process. But, one is witnessing a veritable upheaval, when living labor altogether is cast outside of the real process. This exclusion seems to derive from capitalism to the extent that it is its own aim—the production of surplus value—which requires the continual decrease of necessary labor. And this decrease can only be obtained through the increasing automation of the real process and the considerable increase of instrumental and technological devices. Capitalism thus stimulates the development of technology, since it is the only means that allows it to make labor more productive and to continually decrease the amount of labor needed.

But the possibility of an unlimited development of technology cannot be situated in capitalism itself nor in the new purpose that it introduced into the process. Instead, it is situated in technology itself, and more originally, in Galilean science. By bringing about the dramatic rise of the natural sciences, Galilean science allows for the construction of these instrumental devices that are increasingly elaborate and complex. The conception of these devices is based exclusively on the theoretical knowledge acquired by the sciences. Its reality is homogenous with the physical processes that are the correlate of their knowledge. In the whole universe as it is understood, science isolates certain sequences of phenomena, and it is also able to trigger their starting point. Technological devices are nothing other than this set of processes. The rigorous theoretical definition of them authorizes the programming, deployment, and operation.

That is the principle behind the technical-capitalist world—the point of confluence between capitalism and technology—but it is also the point of their divergence and their contradiction. Capitalism gave rise to an extraordinary development of technology. Its purpose was to increase surplus labor and surplus value by decreasing the amount of necessary labor. This extreme development of instrumental technological devices in the real process of production can indeed be called for by the imperative of development; it can only be introduced because Galilean science already made it possible. The search for money has always taken place. Capitalism simply liberated it. It was only able to change the face of the Earth because the conditions for this change were already established: by Galilean science, by the prodigious rise of the physical-mathematical knowledge of the material world, and by technology which is the unification of this knowledge with the world.

Yet, technological-scientific development does not only make capitalism possible; it also condemns capitalism to death. For capitalism only took hold of the new technological possibilities opened up by science with the aim of producing more value and money. But the exchange value has its origin in the living labor that the technological process irreversibly excludes from the real process as it invades this process and comes to merge with it. Increasingly deprived of living labor and of the subjective force of life, the real process becomes unable to create exchange value, money, and capital. It becomes unable to support an economic process that is only constituted of values. With the gradual disappearance of these values, it too is in effect deprived of its own substance. When subjectivity is excluded from the real process, this is what becomes impossible in the economic process: its very existence.

The huge contradiction that is undermining the world today thus does not come from capitalism alone. Capitalism does indeed display its own contradictions: the growing role of surplus labor in relation to necessary labor, that is to say, in relation to wages brought into the marketplace. Without finding a sufficient amount of money there, many commodities will be unable to realize their exchange value—they will find no buyer. This is how capitalism encounters the constitutive aporia of the market economy: by copying the real process with an economic process, it opened the way to their potential conflict. A use value can only fulfill its function and change into consumption, if its exchange value is honored and exchanged for another identical value or for an equivalent amount of money. But the dissociation of the two processes—where each, at least partly, follows its own logic—renders the correspondence of the use value and exchange value uncertain. Yet this correspondence was at the basis of the invention of the exchange value and of the distinction between them.

With the emergence of Galilean technology and the unlimited extension of its reign—unlimited in the sense that its development takes place as an auto-development and no longer encounters any limit or purpose outside of itself—the difficulties that seem to be tied to the market economy and capitalism take on fantastic proportions. By eliminating subjectivity from the real process of production that has become a technological process, it tends to suppress value; that is to say, the possibility for products to be exchanged and to fulfill their vital purpose. *An entirely automated process and a high-definition technology can produce use values in unlimited amounts but no exchange value*—if we push this exclusion of living labor to the extreme, although it is, of course, only an underlying tendency (*tendancielle*). The imbalance between an increasing amount of technological production of use values and an increasingly weak subjective production of exchange values is not merely a case study or the representation of a tendency whose actual realization would remain problematic. It creates a situation that is already largely the one that we are witnessing—if at least we know how to detect in it the certain signs of its own future.

This is a crisis situation. It is attributed to capitalism, even though it is only the result of techno-science. It is characterized by the impossibility of selling what is produced. Everywhere there is a plethora of goods. This plethora itself is nothing, compared to the virtual plethora inscribed potentially in the almost limitless capacities of the technological system of production. At the same time, there is a lack of the money that would allow individuals to acquire these goods and make use of them. All of the food that cannot be put on the market, all the houses, vehicles, engines, and other kinds of products that cannot be built! "One can" identify the capacity of production through the technological process. Unfortunately, there is no outlet for it; there is no money in the hands of the actual buyers. The vast reserves of accumulated capital are literally nothing in comparison with the use values that the technological process allows to be mass produced. They are nothing, either, with regard to the needs of millions of human beings who are condemned to slums, to deprivation, and to hunger.

The classic crises of capitalism that result from the discrepancy between the mass of manufactured products and insufficient amounts of money in the hands of the workers are only the early warning signs of a permanent crisis. No temporary measure can conjure it away, because it does not get to its principle. Because this is only a tendency (*tendanciel*), it still remains hidden even when its effects are felt more harshly and more widely. This principle is the principle of the market economy; it is the project of appraising and distributing an ever-growing number of products in terms of an exchange value that, in its decline, becomes less able to fulfill its function. The effects of this growing disproportion between use values and exchange values can be recognized through multiple signs. They can be recognized in flourishing businesses as well as in the world desolated by poverty and unemployment. Today the problem for business is to sell or to find market opportunities. This is why the "salesperson" prevails over the engineer and the teaching of marketing prevails over the traditional schools where, through mathematical and physical knowledge, they train those who will have the task of building the new process of production, technology itself.

But there is something even more extraordinary than this recent impossibility for humans find themselves unable to consume what they produce. Note that this impossibility does not concern the consumption of what is superfluous but often what is absolutely necessary. Up to now, we have considered real production as the production of use values, whereas the economic production of exchange value only accompanied it, even though it constantly disturbed it. Let's set aside the latter since it tends to disappear and ceases to occur as the elimination of living labor is pursued. The most decisive trait of the real process leading toward complete automation and thus to an identification with technology, *is the fact that it no longer produces use values, or rather, it produces use values of a new and completely strange type*. The use that had always defined them has totally changed. Up to now, "use" meant the use for life. Wheat was grown and bread was baked in order to be eaten, wine to be drunk, clothes to be worn in order to protect from heat or cold, to protect one's modesty or to express beauty. In short, it was life in the sense that we understand it—the phenomenological life of the living individual—and it alone that prescribed the one and only conceivable purpose of action. And this purpose was not something placed in front of it and separated from it like a target, as an ideal. It was carried out in life itself, in its suffering and enjoying subjectivity.

When Galilean technology invades the real process and reduces it to an objective device, it is not only living labor that is eliminated but also the use value in the sense of a value-for-life. Precisely when production is totally transformed, this is why one sees that with the exchange of the subjective force of living labor for an objective complex of machines and high-powered machines, subjectivity also disappears from the other end of the process. It ceases to be its goal. Production is no longer constituted by use values in the sense of objects that are useful to life and can be consumed by it. But what indeed can one produce that is not for life, its use, or its needs? The technological process itself becomes the goal. Production finds its reality in it, in the set of material devices out of which it is made. And in fact, this is what gets created today: new conductors, new materials, new energy processes for these high-powered machines. Production is at the same time identified with them and devoted to them. When the operation of production is reduced to the performance of a physical process, products become nothing more than the elements of this process. They have no other end than to be integrated into it.

A process of production whose operation is reduced to the functioning of a material device and whose product is only constituted of the objective and material elements of this device—this is a process in which nothing remains of life; this is a dead process.

Here a terrifying truth is revealed to us. *To the theoretical negation of the living individual in Marxism and in the regimes that lay claim to it, there corresponds the factual elimination of the living individual in the technical-capitalist system. In this system, capitalism is itself on the way to disappearing to the benefit of a complete liberation of technology and its auto-development.* This situation is no longer only a tendency (*tendancielle*): it is established in the "liberal economies" that are juxtaposed with the agonizing socialist regimes. The former like the latter are mourning for life. Death thus has two faces. Let's scrutinize them more closely.

8 DEATH AND POLITICS

The theoretical negation of the individual makes Marxism one of the pure forms of fascism. It shapes a conception of the political that is all the more significant to the extent that it can be found in related ways in the modern democracies whose opposition to totalitarian regimes thus comes to appear problematic. In any case, the question of the essence of the political is tied to human nature. The political upheavals in the East and notably the abrupt conversion from communist regimes to liberal democracies make the clarification of these connections more urgent than ever.

First of all, it should be understood that there is no more "politics" in nature than there is an economic reality, properly speaking. It is indeed difficult to conceive a human group lacking any form of organization or hierarchy—without any organization, there would be no coherence of the actions necessary to the group's survival. But one should not rush to call this spontaneous organization "political," any more than the act of hunting a deer or fleeing from danger can be called "economics." Just as the economy presupposes the copying of all practical activities by a specific world of idealities that can ensure its operation, likewise the political projects a horizon of understanding—a sense of another order—that goes beyond these practical activities.

As with the economy which begins from the original subjective activities of need and work, one must therefore identify the Act that creates this specific dimension of politics. We naïvely believe that politics is inherent in the things which have to do with human beings, just as we naïvely believe that the price of sugar is contained in a piece of sugar. The founding Act of the "political" is the act by which consciousness confers onto a series of facts a meaning that concerns all the individuals belonging to a given group. That is to say that it is taken to be an affair of all—*a public affair*. This act of consciousness creates a meaning that is an ideality, and its content "being the affair of all" is ideal. This ideal content, understood as a "public affair," defines the political as such. It is the political essence.

From this origin of the political essence, it follows that there is no autonomy. Not only does it presuppose the act of consciousness that has engendered this meaning, in addition its content—this sense of being an affair common to all—necessarily refers beyond consciousness itself and to those for whom it is an affair, that is, to the living individuals and to the many subjective activities in which their lives are produced. The content of public affairs is these many activities. We have already encountered their infinitely varied and complex unity under the heading of "social praxis." Inasmuch as its content is drawn from this network of interconnected activities, public reality has no other reality than these activities, than the essentially individual and subjective reality of life.

But, does not a public affair stand in opposition to what is each time the affair of a particular individual? Whether I might choose to live with this woman or to leave her, to practice this profession or some other one, this is my business and not that of a commune or a county. But what accounts for the personal character of an individual's life cannot be limited to these big decisions that punctuate a life and shape its course. Each action of daily life, each effort of labor, and each urge of need is marked by the indelible stamp of individuality. It is an individual affair that is particular and private; it is moved by its own motives and obeys its "individual interests." It would be absurd to oppose public affairs with activities of this kind. Even though they are always the affairs of a particular individual and take place in one's own life, they nonetheless form the substance of social life. Is it not also the affair of all—of all these lives that are lived and experience in the irreducibility of their singular subjectivity—of their praxis and their pathos?

What results from this initial analysis of the political is its referential character. It is impossible to conceive of a public affair that does not refer to the life of individuals as its only real content. In this respect, the political essence does not have any autonomy. Like economic reality, it does not exist on its own. Just as economic laws cannot be rendered intelligible within the economic field, likewise the laws or norms of politics cannot be derived from an explanation or criteria that are properly political.

In particular, it is necessary to guard against a political interpretation of the definition of politics. To say that public affairs are the affairs of each and every one is self-evident to the point of seeming tautological. What is also self-evident is to immediately give a political sense to this proposition. This would be to put it in play within the political field, whereas this definition should cast us outside of this field, to the non-political site of life.

Politically, to say that public affairs are the affairs of all means that everyone has a say about how to conduct public affairs. It is in relation to whether or not this requirement is satisfied that different types of regimes can be distinguished and that a hierarchy can be established in which some are praised and others condemned. In the regimes that are praised, the individual has the right and the means, as a citizen, to participate in deliberations relating to the public interest, to the definition of it and to the decisions that follow from this definition. In the regimes that are condemned, this right is taken away from the individual. The former regimes are democracies in which the concept of the "republic" is honored, for democracy defines public affairs as public, as affairs that are the affairs of everyone and debated publicly by everyone. The latter regimes are dictatorships that, in various ways, deny the citizen the right to participate in the *res publica* and thereby contradict this concept. It is naïve to think about the events in the East in light of this opposition between democracy and dictatorship. What matters to us for the time being is to understand that the question of the participation or non-participation of the individual in public affairs—with all the different political responses that are brought to this question—points to a prior problem. This problem concerns the existence of a properly political dimension. It presupposes the opening up of this political field, its intro-duction, or, rather, its genesis from life. This genesis is carried out through the mediation of an act of consciousness. It thinks a certain number of activities, that are in themselves subjective and individual, as the affairs of all. Let's show this with a concrete example.

Take an irrigation or water conveyance plan brought forward for deliberation by a political assembly, say, a municipal council. It is to the extent that the plan is discussed by a political assembly of this kind that it becomes a political affair. But from where does the assembly derive its political character? It is from being assigned to deal with this kind of affair. The institution of an assembly, of a political organism, of political institu-tions as a whole and thus of the State itself, results from this aim. In the regard of this aim, and as a result of it, particular affairs are able to appear as public. This aim constitutes the act that gives birth to the political. Whatever its historical origin, empirical content, and changes may be, the State—which is the totality of political institutions—refers to this transcen-dental birth of the political essence. The State is only possible in light of it.

This aim is the concern of municipal council members when they debate an irrigation plan. It is in light of this aim that the plan can appear to them as the business of the community. However, *this entrance into the political aim does not change anything about the affair in question.* In spite of the presentation of its documents and its arrival on the council's agenda, the irrigation plan refers immediately to reality—to the subjective reality of life. In sum, it includes two aspects. The first aspect involves the labor—the number of hours of labor necessary for digging the ditches, laying the pipes, or even making them, for the maintenance and use of the machinery, etc. The number of hours is the quantifiable objective equivalent of something of another order: the real labor of those who are at the worksite or in the factory.

The second aspect of the plan involves the state of affairs that will result from this labor and justifies the undertaking: this irrigation, this water, and these cultivars. These use values will be consumed in life and only have reality in life. Under both aspects—whether it is the execution of the labor or the result of it—we are only dealing with life. With the entrance into the political and the arrival on the agenda of the council, once again, nothing is changed about the essential subjectivity of life. There is no magical transubstantiation as a result of which what is hollowed out in the silent suffering of one's effort or in the enjoyment of consumption, would be offered up suddenly to a regard and would then be there for each and every one. What is there for each and every one—right in front of them on the table—is only the plan, the document. It is only an objective equivalent that, like the economic entities to which it refers, points back to an invisible subjectivity. In the end, irrigation, water and agricultural products can only have a sense for it alone.

The greatest danger occurs when one denies this essentially referential character of politics, and, more profoundly, the proper nature of what it refers to—the radical subjectivity of the life. It is only experienced each time in the form of a Self that is irreducible to any other. Or even more simply, the danger is that one ceases to perceive this at all. This concealment of the founding sense of life and of living individuals occurs in Marxism, and we have shown how it occurs. Starting from the moment when the individual is absorbed into the social class, when its properties are only understood as objects and ultimately as the objective properties of this class, starting from the moment when these properties and their laws are what define reality and when reality is henceforth understood as "economic and social," and as objective in nature, the individual is stripped of everything that belongs to it. One's experience of oneself in suffering or satisfaction is no longer what matters, nor is it what defines true being—it is only an effect. Even when the lot of the individual is considered, its being is perceived, evaluated, and understood on the basis of another reality than its own. To act on it, it is necessary to act on another reality than its own. Moreover, this action on the individual has only become possible because it is determined completely by another, objective reality that makes it possible to arrange it in this or that way. For, all action is of this sort and consists in the objective modification of a state of affairs that is itself objective.

We are already familiar with this objective reality that is foreign to the individual. It must henceforth be the theme of the analysis and that on which it will act. Under the traditional Marxist heading of "economic and social reality," it is the set of objective equivalents that have been created to correspond with the invisible subjectivity of the individual. This correspondence occurs when it measures the subject's action for the sake of exchanging products. Seen in light of the theory of the genealogy of social classes and of economic reality, this idea—that living individuals are determined by a set of abstractions that have replaced their lives so that they can be known—is quite simply absurd. However, the undivided reign of objective knowledge and its correlate—namely, a reality that is defined by its objectivity and that is valued in this way—becomes widely extended. This gives rise to the illusion that the individual is determined entirely by the objective reality in which it is found, and the individual is increasingly identified by means of equivalents. This illusion continues to gain ground. Inasmuch as they are integrated with the Galilean model of a radically objective science, the economic and social sciences have no other designs today than to conform to this model.

Under this socio-economic interpretation of the individual, what happens to the political essence, then? One of the major themes of Marxism—which was retained from Marx's teachings—is the reduction of politics to economics, which is understood as what really underlies it. In this regard, politics appears as a mere expression of economic reality. Political struggles, for example, only reflect class struggles, and class struggles themselves derive from the structure of productive forces and their evolution. In addition, politics is defined by the aim for the universal. But, politics also usually turns out to be a mask. It deals with public affairs that are supposed to be the affairs of those who it claims to serve, but in reality they are only the affairs of the capitalists. The government itself is, as we see today in Japan and elsewhere, only "the administrative council for the high affairs of the bourgeoisie."

In spite of the devaluation that it undergoes from this reductionist perspective, it is necessary to understand why the political nonetheless takes on a preponderate role for the Marxists. It is necessary to understand how and why it defines, in their eyes, a privileged mode of life, and at the extreme limit, the only mode of life that gives sense to life. To recall, this is the case because for Marxism the individual is nothing. Unable to follow Marx's steps back to the foundation, the Marxist analysis stops with economic reality and immediately takes it as reality. It does not break down this reality into the subjective life of living individuals, on the one side, and the economic determinations that are only "representatives" of it, on the other side. Instead, it takes the latter—the set of ideal abstractions of the economy—as the real constituents of a system in which individual lives are only the effects. The individual is thus emptied of its substance to the benefit of the economic regulations in which it is held. What remains of the personal—pain, boredom, effort, sickness—is put, in turn, through a process of objectification where these subjective modalities are transformed into a number of social features that are determined by class and that are objective like it. At the end of this "analysis," everything stands on its head. The individual is really nothing more than the site of objective properties and characteristics that determine the basis of its being—the self is only this objectified basis.

What can be done for this individual who is no longer anything but the point of intersection and plaything of economic and social processes? What can be done to understand them so they can be acted on? If the objective conditions of history and society are the conditions of the individual's own existence, what can be done to transform these conditions in such a way that they transform the individual's existence? This is the political aim: it takes the life of the individual as a set of economic and social conditions and seeks to understand them. It necessarily raises itself up above the limited point of view of the egoistic individual to open onto an objective and universal truth. It apprehends all problems in their generality, as public affairs. For the individual who just had its individuality negated and has been dismissed from its personal life as well as from the right to have one, politics is thus the sole means of overcoming its insignificance and of becoming more than a grain of sand on the beach. It is the sole means of regaining the possibility for action.

This possibility could only be political, like the aim that underlies it. On the one hand, it presupposes a regard that embraces the totality of conditions necessary for a transformation with a collective meaning— the irrigation of the community or the settlement of land. On the other hand, the accomplishment of the objectives perceived and prescribed by the political aim implies a capacity for action that is on its level, and the isolated individual does not contain in itself the power to change the objective conditions in which he or she lives. A more important group of individuals would not be able to do it, either. In order to be possible on the social level, action must change its level. Its principle can no longer be an individual action, whatever may be the number of those who participate in it. Only a social force is able to provide an answer to the political aim of public affairs, and this force is the force of a class. The individual members of a class are no longer joined together in terms of individual, non-organic, and variable characteristics: action is motivated by social characteristics. The coherence that they confer on action is the coherence of the class; it is the class itself.

And it is here that politics rejoins History. It has ceased to be a mere superstructure, the evanescent reflection running along the surface of economic phenomena. Precisely because it has economic phenomena in its encompassing view, it sees that in the objective situation they are the forces that determine it and make it what it is. By inviting everyone to rejoin these great powers residing in History, it also gives everyone the possibility of going beyond their own derisory fate and of participating in building a new world. This is how political consciousness overturns its own initial situation of dependence. By identifying with class and its struggle, the *homo politicus* is able to rejoin the true agents of History and to become one of them.

All things considered, this revaluation of the political requires three conditions. The first condition is, in any case, the lowering or the nullification of the individual left to itself: its egoistic interests, its modest ambitions, and its congenital powerlessness. The second condition is the existence of a social reality that is higher than it, and it must go beyond itself in order to identify with this movement and with the breath of History. There is some ambiguity in Marxism concerning this supra-individual reality to which the individual is joined in the ethical movement of "self-surpassing." It is partly an economic determinism that is analogous to natural determinism and that is hardly more exalting than natural determinism. But, it is partly about History, which is invested with existential categories that are much more prestigious; these categories are borrowed from Hegelianism, from the theosophy of Jacob Boehme, and, through them, from Christianity itself.

Exposed schematically and made visible through the Archetype of Christ, this self-surpassing is the idea that one can only attain salvation through death and that one can only attain happiness through suffering. In dialectical terms, that is to say that each thing emerges from its contrary, that the negative is the condition for the positive, that the antithesis is the condition for the thesis, the obstacle is the condition for its resolution, and that contradiction defines the structure of every conceivable process. This determines the structure of history. To take the most significant example, it is plain to see how the proletariat echoes the history of Christ. By falling into worse and worse misery ("the gradual pauperization of the proletariat") and by assuming the fate of humanity as a whole, it is the proletariat that can lead humanity to its salvation. Situated at the core of the historical process, the contradiction allows for the introduction of the totality of economic contradictions that were raised scientifically through the critique of political economy. Because it intermingles with "dialectical and historical materialism" in its claim to be objective science, this messianic conception of an initially wounded but ultimately triumphant Desire—this affective history is nothing other than the history of life itself; secretly, this history receives its ability to fascinate from life—has enabled Marxism to exercise an impact for more than a century on so many different minds, whether they are scientific or believers.

The third condition for the revaluation of politics is the most important one, but it is also the most dangerous one. It does not only concern Marxism and the totalitarian regimes which were constructed in light of its principles but also the democracies with which one would like to replace them, especially in the Eastern bloc countries. Is it a mere chance if this third condition leads us back to the first one—that is, to the devaluation of the individual—and calls on us to rethink it? This calls for a rethinking, at the same time, of the oppositions that have always governed political theory: the oppositions between individual/society, singular/universal, private interests/public affairs. In short, these oppositions lead each individual to seem insignificant in relation to the collectivity that dominates it, and into which the individual must be integrated. What, in the end, is the basis for this dichotomy which is ever-present but usually remains unreflected?

The political is the aim for the universal. It takes into account the various activities of particular individuals in order to consider them as a public affair. It is only once they are grasped in light of this unifying synthesis that these various activities can become effective and yield coherent results. But the aim itself—which consists of considering everything as political—is detached from the prior view of the world in which every consideration and every possible aim are inscribed. The light that the political aim sheds on the unified praxis of individuals is not its own; it is the light of the world; it is the horizon of visibility on the basis of which each thing is shown to us in such a way that we are able to see it and know it. The political has an essential phenomenological meaning, but this meaning is a borrowed one. Nonetheless, it rebounds back to the political and gives it the power of clarification and of putting into perspective which is identified with rationality. Through its opposition to particular interests, divergent egoisms, and a multitude of anarchic, blind forces, it comes to dominate them. The light of the political requires them to be directed toward a common goal, instead of tearing one another apart in the pointless war of all against all.

What are these blind forces and these anarchic, divergent interests?

They are the forces and interests of the individual. The revaluation of the political is accompanied with the devaluation of the individual and presupposes it. This ethical-political hierarchy elevates the political and lowers the individual; it subordinates the singular to the aim for the universal. This does not result merely from one value judgment that could be contrasted with another one, instead it refers to a prior and essential hierarchy on the phenomenological level. This hierarchy is introduced between two modes of appearing: *the mode of appearing of life which experiences itself in the silent embrace of its pathos and as a pathos, in contrast with the appearing of the world, which is the horizon of visibility where the political aim is fulfilled.*

Truly speaking, it is not really a hierarchy that is in question here, not even an inverted hierarchy. Political thought simply ignores the labor of life within us, inasmuch as it is given to itself in its pure subjectivity. This is why political thought identifies the action of an individual who receives its own essence from life with a brutal or "blind" action. Because it is found to lack every phenomenological property, individual activity is "blind." Because it is blind, individual activity cannot lead on its own to any positive result. The competition between several individual actions would be impossible, if it did not have the aim for the universal or the light of the political added onto them and regulating them from above so that they harmonize and connect—"the light of the State," as Marx ironized in his polemic against Hegel.[1] To the extent that life is misunderstood with regard to its own essence—which is to feel oneself—and to the extent that it is deprived of its power to bring about revelation, this power is henceforth confined to the world and to it alone. Everything is confined to the light of the world where the political regards all that exists as something that is there for each and every one—as a public affair.

The ancient City is the concrete historical form in which the political is identified with the phenomenality of the world. It draws its power and prestige from the ancient City. The City is nothing but the world on the human scale, the world of all those who are able to perceive it together from the same point. The City is this space of light where the actions of the men and women who live within its walls are manifested. Illuminated by this light, their actions become harmonious and are integrated in the City in a beautiful totality about which the romantics. This light of the world allows them to be shown to everyone and to be there for everyone. It is on this basis that public affairs acquire their proper determination: publicity. It is an affair that everyone can see, and they are related to it in an aim that posits it. As such, it is accessible to all: the public affair, the *res publica*, the re-public. The public-ness of public affairs is the basis of its generality. It is to the extent that is seen by everyone, in the light of the City, that it can be the affair of everyone: a public affair. The phenomenon of the world is thus the basis of the political: being-in-the-world, being-with-others, and forming a political community with them. Each individual action acquires its legitimacy from the political community, inasmuch as it belongs to it. It is shown and can only be shown in it.

This phenomenological meaning of the political—its ability to be shown to everyone—is the basis of what I call its hypostasis. It is considered as an autonomous reality and as the only true reality in which individuals can participate. Individuals draw their own being from it, to the extent that they have any being at all. This phenomenological valorization of the political—whose immediate consequence is the ontological inflation of the political essence—expresses the great deficiency of Western thought. This is really a phenomenological deficiency. It is the operative belief that, when it comes to phenomenality, there is nothing but the phenomenality of the world. Everything that exists is manifest to us in the light of this horizon of visibility, notably the interconnected actions which are the substance of a society. To the benefit of this spectacle and everything that is shown in it, everything that has to do with life and its own original mode of appearing—this way of feeling oneself in a subjectivity that is foreign to the spectacle of the world—is abolished: the individuals from whom these actions occur, the subjectivity which refers actions back to individuals and turns them into individual actions in principle. Individual actions are indeed shown in the light of the world and of the City, but only after they have undergone a process of objectification. This process always conceals what is most proper to them; namely, the subjective pathos which makes each one the action of a singular individual.

This objectification transforms all of these lives into empirical individuals who are seen from the outside and cut off from their acting and suffering interiority. This produces another illusion. For, individuals are never isolated: traversed by life and its drives, individuals are thrust toward one another. This force of life within each individual pushes each one to join with others. It constitutes the foundation of every conceivable community as a community of drives (*pulsionelle*). Each one is thus with another not only due to one's desires but through all one's affective modes—sympathy, pity, love, hate, resentment, solitude. And, first of all, one is with the other in the silent being-with that unites the child with its mother, but this affect retains the same dynamic and emotional status throughout one's life and history.

This original being-in-common unfolds in life and draws the force of its drive from life, but it is appropriated by political thought. According to it, it is the consideration of public affairs as the affairs of all that leads them to gather together around the affairs of all. One can only reconnect with others through the aim for the universal, inasmuch as it is a way of going beyond oneself and leaving oneself. With these shared spaces, everything is turned upside down once again. For if an actual experience of the other can take place, it is only insofar as I experience the other in me, as a modification of my life, my desire, or my love. And if public affairs can be sought politically as the affairs of everyone, then this can only be the case to the extent that this really is in oneself. It must refer to the life of each of those whom it concerns and thus to the community of life in which all living beings exist. Without this original, pre-political, and pre-social community, no common project could ever come to exist. For, no project of this kind can be formed independently from its rootedness in the organic structure of desire and action. This is how being-in-common came to be embodied in the living subjectivity of individuals well before political thought turned it into the object of its aim in the form of public affairs. Instead of being the result of this aim or being constituted in this aim, the community of life is its cause and its condition.

Totalitarianism is the result of the hypostasis of the political and the correlative lowering of life as well as the individual. This term does not refer to one type of political regime that can be contrasted with other regimes. Its threat looms over any conceivable regime in which the political is taken as the essential and in which the concealment of life's own way of appearing extends its reign over human beings, thereby determining a phase of their history. When politics appears on the center of the stage and claims to direct the plot, dangerous times are announced—the time of revolution, terror, and death. The horror of such times ought not hide their internal logic. For if public affairs are all that matters, if they are placed above the individual, and if they claim the right to their needs over those of the individual, then public affairs can also suppress the individual. The individual is considered to exist only in it, for it and by it. The individual is nothing without it.

Such murders are usually only carried out symbolically, in the form of a political theory or philosophy. It suffices to share this with as many as possible for a political regime, such as communism, to be justified ideologically and continue to live its precarious existence as an ideology or symbol. But things sometimes become more serious. Faced with obscure resistance from the life that it represses, the political essence needs to prove its usurped reality. Here the negation of the particular occurs for real. For the political is the universal; it is motivated by and results from the negation of the singular individual. And this opens up a properly political era in history, where reality becomes really political. It is fulfilled in political murder, which is the murder of the individual in the name of the political essence.

Totalitarianism contains these latent presuppositions, and they are actualized in times of revolution and terror. Like any other regime, it cannot entirely misunderstand reality, that is, the reality of the living individuals whose praxis constitutes the social substance. The political essence unavoidably refers to this subjectivity, but political thought will abolish it at the very moment when it pretends to recognize it. This evasion occurs under the cover of the cherished concept of politics: the concept of the people. This reveals the disturbing kinship that links totalitarianism and democracy. For, although the notion of the people seeks to be inclusive of the totality of individuals, it is also no one. This notion surreptitiously abolishes the most decisive feature of life, namely, the fact that it is always an individual life. Since life only exists in the form of a particular individual, it is life that is eliminated with this elimination of the individual. The people then receive its true name: the negation of all possible life, death. That is the reason why it was possible in the name of the people—and very logical—to carry out so many crimes: the notion of the people is foreign to life and to the individual. Once it is taken on its own—as an autonomous reality—it is ranked higher than the reality of the individuals who make it up, and it is seen independently from their reality. Clearly, the concept of the people is the political equivalent of the concepts of class and of society that were criticized previously. It presents the same ontological vacuity, the same powerlessness to exercise any effective action whatsoever. Just like the concept of society, the concept of the people has never been noticed in the process of laboring or of performing a surgical procedure. To do those things, as Marx said, human beings are necessary.

The ontological vacuity of the concept of the people spills over to the concept of democracy and strikes at its core. In a democracy, it is the people who govern. Unfortunately, "the people" does not exist: it cannot govern any more than it can labor in a field or plant in it. The concept of democracy is thus a lure. It is the most extraordinary lure which has ever been invented by humans in order to abuse themselves and others. This lure is dangled today in front of the stupified gaze of all the nations who together seek to build Europe. But, this fact does not change anything about the ontological mystification on which it is based; it only makes it more dangerous.

If the people, like society or social classes, does not exist on its own as an autonomous reality but only as a concept whose sole objective reference is the multiple subjectivities of "living individuals," then its political meaning is completely changed, or rather, annulled. In other words, reality itself has ceased to be political. Governing is thus no longer up to the people but to the multiple individuals for which the people is only a name. For it is precisely then that the hypostasis of the political is put to an end; the democratic or totalitarian illusion is the permanent possibility of political murder and terror. The political problem is posed at last in concrete terms—but unfortunately it is posed in the form of an aporia.

The only positive sense of the concept of democracy is its non-political sense, because it refers to the non-political reality of society, that is, to living individuals. Its positive sense is thus as follows: it is up to these individuals and to all of them to govern. But this is not possible, and that is the aporia. This aporia gave rise to the invention of the political, just as the impossibility of measuring living labor gave rise to the invention of the economy. Since not everyone can actually govern and take part in deliberations over the affairs of the State, they will do it through the intermediary of representatives. By being elected by them in place of them, these representatives will legislate or decide in their name within the various organisms established for this end and which are the various political powers.

Political representation—which is characteristic of the republic and of democracy—thus refers public affairs back to their non-political foundation. But, in so doing, it puts something else in the place of this non-political foundation—it no longer consists of all living individuals but only their delegates. This is how the affairs of everyone become *politically* the affairs of some. Public affairs, when treated as political and universal, fall under the contrary determination of being reserved to a caste, namely, to the "political class." When democracy is replaced by a totalitarian dictatorship, one nomenclature takes the place of another one—although they are not the same. *It is not when it was the private affair of an individual closed in on its effort, its pain, or joy that it was particular—it was the affair of life, of the infinite life that flows through us and obstinately pursues its hidden goals—it is precisely when it becomes political that it turns into the affairs of some; they present it and continue to present it as the affairs of all.* This is why there is hypocrisy in every political regime in principle—in communist dictatorships as well as in the democracies which will follow it in the East.

To this perversion which corrupts politics from its very birth can be added a second one. This perversion is more serious because it affects the very content of public affairs. As we have seen, it does not change anything about the specificity of public affairs, if it is considered *as* general and, in light of the State, *as* political. To the extent that its substance is located in life, it is only a particular affair: irrigation, coastal management, or the management of a museum. These define areas of an educational curriculum. They are always derived from a particular competency possessed by specific individuals: it is the affair of urban planners, agricultural engineers, university professors, etc. The fact that it becomes political and is considered to be political means that it passes into other hands. It passes into the hands of those who have been chosen or have chosen themselves. But, they lack the required aptitude. This is how the choice of a monument—for example, the choice of its placement and style—comes to result from the decision of a political council and not from those who, as artists and creators, would have expertise about it. Even worse than the dialectical inversion by which the affairs of all become those of a few, there is an abyss that separates the formal political decision from the concrete content of the affair which it handles. This concrete content is always an affair of life. For this reason, the truth of political power must be disclosed as a principle of arbitrariness and incompetence.

The incompetence of the political can be seen within each of the organisms that it puts into place and culminates in the administration. Under the pretext of defending the public interest, the nature of the administration is to always place its problems, its methods, and its interests—in short, its own bureaucratic aims—over the living aims of individual undertakings. In relation to them, it acts as an external constraint and as a force of death. The so-called bureaucratic regimes have disastrous consequences for the economic activity of a country; that is to say, for all of the individual activities forming its basic outline. But, these regimes cannot be distinguished politically—for instance, as totalitarian or democratic regimes. In these regimes, the political principle prevails to the point of claiming to rule over the entire domain of the economic, social, and cultural life of a country.

The prejudice that the political inflicts on life is thus the same principle everywhere. It is due less to the particular nature of the political institutions imposed here or there than to the distortion that the political as such makes everything alive undergo. This distortion is twofold: it consists first in the claim to make public and to expose in the light of the world something that can only deploy its essence in the invisible subjectivity of life. Second, as a result of the first distortion, it consists of the replacement of the affairs of living individuals by supposedly public affairs that would be substantially different from them. The political perversion thereby rejoins the more general perversion that we have denounced throughout the analyses in this book. This perversion is a substitution that puts something which is not alive in place of what is alive; it hangs a mortal threat over life.

CONCLUSION: THE RENDEZVOUS IN SAMARKAND

The trembling servant threw himself at the feet of his master: I beg you, Master, to allow me to leave!—Why are you frightened?—I met death at the marketplace, and she looked at me—Where are you going?—To Samarkand: I will get lost in the crowd and she will not find me.

The master went to find death at the marketplace: Why did you cause such fear in my servant?—Me? I did not seek any harm. I have a rendezvous with him in Samarkand.[1]

Our attempt to understand the profound political changes occurring in the Eastern bloc countries first led us to recognize their true cause, namely, the economic failure of socialism. This failure might seem to belong to the economic order and to be expressed in a state of impoverishment that links communist regimes to underdeveloped countries. But, here is a strange fact. Deeper reflection suggests the following observation: it is not ultimately the economic regime itself, in its objective definition, that leads to this collapse. One can indeed imagine a system based on the socialization of the means of production that, by contrast, would turn out to be a source of prosperity and even of abundance. Admittedly, this was Marx's dream. This abundance ought to resolve all of the problems, the thorniest one being the problem of social justice. Better than the theoreticians who claimed to follow him but did not know all of his work, Marx understood very well that this type of social justice is only a lure because it is impossible in principle. The only solution to it would be an overabundance that would render the question of sharing pointless.

This point of view implies an essential truth that is quite foreign to socialist ideology. Individuals—those whom we have called living individuals throughout this book—and individuals alone create the wealth of societies. The disappearance of wealth also derives from them and from them alone. And it is here that the economic bankruptcy of socialism requires us to look for its cause outside of the sphere of the economy and in the individuals themselves. If communist regimes today, after a half century or more of existence, have a track record of catastrophe, this is for the simple reason that no one does anything there and no one wants to do anything else there. And one can understand why Brezhnev, as it has been said, placed all of his hopes on computers. These magical instruments were supposed to take over the role of all social activity, while individuals would be able to peacefully drink their glasses of vodka with their legs crossed and slumped in front of their television screens.

The question comes up again: in communist regimes, why do individuals no longer want to do anything? We have answered that it is due to social justice. Social justice is injustice itself, because it is absolutely unjust to pay someone who is incompetent and does nothing the same wage as someone who performs, through effort and pain, a productive and beneficent activity. Life carries within itself the true justice, and thus it knows the true price, the price of pain and effort. They are never wrong in any case about themselves—the result is that they too decide to fold their own arms so that nothing is done any more. Impoverishment occurs as the inevitable result of social justice, and it acts in turn on its own conditions; it reinforces them and redoubles them. What is the point of working for nothing—for a wage that gives one the right to stand in endless waiting lines for a little bit of bread or some frozen potatoes? It is better to seize hold of them directly, without working or standing in lines, through some type of trafficking or pillage. Along with impoverishment, this is how the theoretical negation of life and its irrepressible interests gives rise within life itself to the most savage and brutal behaviors.

We then encounter the most serious error of Marxism: the devaluation of the individual. All of its setbacks and all of its violence flow from this error. If life is the only power, the only force, and the only reality, then it suffices to consider it as a negligible quantity in order to find the world of desolation that communism shows everywhere. In Marxism, the under-estimation of the principle of all reality is the result of an explicit theoretical process: the replacement of individual living beings by a number of abstractions that claim to hold, in their place, the power to organize society, and, first of all, the power to act—although they are unable to do anything whatsoever on their own. We have denounced the great ideological abstractions—Society, History, social class, the proletariat—and ultimately the Party which claims to represent the proletariat.

In a sense, the negation of reality can only be abstract, like the abstractions with which one seeks to replace reality. In other words, it is impossible to negate life. Life remains through its obstinate will, its unavoidable needs, and its immense Desire. First and foremost, it is the desire to live. The abstractions that are put in place of living individuals cannot have any other substance than them. If one eliminated all individuals, there would no longer be a Society, a History, a people, or classes. Like every doctrine leading toward the devaluation of the individual and especially like all forms of fascism, Marxism is thus faced with the following contradiction: precisely because life defines reality, the negation of life cannot be carried out.

What remains, then, is to realize this pious vow in a partial way. This leads to a series of liquidations of specific individuals. In order to carry out these limited genocides, a criterion of selection must be used. In Marxism, this criterion will be the social class or one of its sub-groups: the bourgeoisie, the petty-bourgeoisie, the holders of privileges like education or culture, the owners of some semblance of a house or even a few cows. The criterion might even be some type of specialized training, not to mention national characteristics. Through the combination of these various characteristics, there results a sub-group like "Polish officers."[2] In other types of fascism, the criterion of selection will be racial or at least supposedly so. In any case, the theoretical possibility of systematic murder is based on the existence of an objective criterion. That is to say that it is based precisely on the substitution of an objective given for the non-objective and non-objectifiable metaphysical reality of the individual in life.

One can then see in its full breadth and in all its horror the abyss that opens up underneath this substitution. Wherever some form of objectivity is put in place of life—in the sense that it claims not to represent it but to actually take its place—the justification of murder is acquired. The discovery of the reign of substitution in its full magnitude gives rise to vertigo. Very noble forms of thought—however removed they might seem to be from the criminal presuppositions that we just exposed—actually have disturbing affinities with them. How can one forget Galileo's decision to exclude all the sensible qualities from our knowledge of the world, along with sensibility, affectivity, and everything else that is subjective in us and that constitutes our own being—to exclude our life?

In this inaugural act of science and modern thought, it is what we are that gets set aside. This type of knowledge might be valid for matter, but it no longer knows anything about subjectivity and no longer has any way to know it. Inasmuch as it claims to submit what we are to this knowledge, the individual gets reduced to what is taught about it in the schools. It is an empirical individual submitted to all of the different objective approaches toward it. Its scientific truth cannot be discovered outside of them. It is a tiny and insignificant bit of the universe that is made up of particles and atoms, molecules, and acid chains—it is the neuronal human. Or, if biology or the human sciences want to be seriously concerned about it, it will be an individual member of an ethnicity or race. Or it will be the social individual defined by its class—although class will eventually be eliminated like the individual. Or it will be the worker in the economy whose abstract labor is quantifiable and qualifiable; it does not matter whether it is performed by one individual or by another one. Physics, chemistry, biology, social, or human sciences, political economy—you know so little about the human! And that is not because you still have a lot of progress to make but because life is not situated where you are looking or within your field of vision.

What a marvel is a political system whose explicit foundation is the birthright of every individual, "human rights!" This must include the right of each one to be fully him or herself and to carry out the grand designs of the life within him or herself. What a model is an economic regime whose principle is the activity of the individual understood as the source of all effectiveness and all wealth! What would be more natural than for such a model to shine today in the eyes of millions of unfortunate people who have been trapped for decades in the socialist paradise of poverty and fear? The opening to the West is not only motivated by economic bankruptcy, or to put it better, *this bankruptcy is not an objective phenomenon.* It is experienced precisely in suffering; it is situated in life and so to speak clothed in its armor. In a way, this bankruptcy acts like life, as an irresistible force that henceforth escapes all control. But can this repressed, threatened, constrained, and furious life actually find what it seeks in the West, namely, itself? Can it find what it seeks in the West—in regimes that are politically democracies and economically capitalism in the current stage of its evolution?

Democracy does not exist. It claims to give power to the people but the people do not exist either—no more than society, History, class, or the proletariat exist. Thank God! If the great *demos* did exist, if democracy were possible, then it would exist literally as a popular democracy, that is to say, as a fascist dictatorship. The same great abstract entity that took the place of individuals would turn back against them at every moment. It would make them march in step, strip them of their possessions, or shoot them—all in the name of the people! This would happen in the same way that individuals have been forced to march in step, have been extorted, or shot in the name of the proletariat. What is the proletariat but the people that has gotten rid of its parasites? The proletariat-people does not only have the right and obligation to eliminate social parasites; it is also against each one of its members. It is against each individual who can claim his or her own power inasmuch as this power is not in the people but precisely in the individual, who was taken as something insignificant, obscure, suspect, and who was nothing on its own. Would not the fabled rendezvous with democracy be a rendezvous in Samarkand?

It is thus important to return to the only acceptable sense of the concept of democracy, that is, to its reference not to the people but to living individuals. The idyllic situation would be an Amazonian tribe holding a general assembly at night in which everyone participates, including women and children, and decides together the date for the next festival at which the sons and daughters of the neighboring tribe will be eaten. But, with that exception, it should be recognized that not "everyone" can govern in an ordinary country of even a modest size. They will then govern through the intermediary of elected delegates and through the mediation of all of the political institutions that make up the State. Once again, this deploys an empire of substitutions, and leads to the establishment of a new nomenclature very similar to the one that was just knocked down. Its characteristics are quite similar: the thirst for power and advantages leads to tenacious disputes among the various factions in the political caste; it leads to hypocrisy and incompetence. The latter characteristics, however, only become principles of government through more general substitutions that engender the political world itself: the substitution of the affairs of life—of everything which is alive and can only live in life—by general affairs that are public and political. They expose its being in the light of the State. They become the business of everyone and everyone is able to see them. But this can occur only if they are emptied of their subjective substance and are no longer the affairs of anyone.

That is why only the members of the political-media caste appear in the spotlight of this public space. Only they have a voice, the right to say what they think, assuming that they think at all. All of the others are reduced to silence, especially those who think, and they undergo the most extraordinary censorship that has ever existed. In the days of the kings of Prussia, Stalin, or Hitler, one at least knew that censorship existed. But today, under the reign of liberty, one no longer even knows about it. This is how the extraordinary ideological conditioning of the whole society— the media and advertising are hammered into almost all of one's mental contents, including one's desires and dreams—takes place all the time and for everyone, including children, but without any critique, without any power of contestation even being able to show its mere existence.

This substitution—that is, the transcription of life into an objectivity where life does not exist—is the origin of the entire economic world.

It would thus be a mistake to contrast free enterprise with centralized planning, as if the former expressed the dynamism of life—its initiatives and its individual responsibilities—in contrast with the weight of bureaucracy and the incompetence of political intervention. It is true that capitalism is based on the living individual. We have shown that the living individual accounts for its force and is also the cause of the revolution that it introduced in human history. Capitalism exploited as much of the subjective labor power as it could. In so doing, it created vast reserves of wealth and money that allowed it to become a moment in the system. If the market economy prevails today over state-based economies, this is certainly not due to the "market" and its so-called free play. The market economy only prevails because—underneath the great fluctuations of the phenomena of production, business, and finance, and underneath the superimposed strata of economic entities that are increasingly distant from their source and increasingly cover it over—there stands the unfailing power of life. What capitalism can still offer positively is due to the power of life and to it alone. Although the power of life is taken into the economic world that it creates, its power is constantly paralyzed by the economic world. For, this world is not simply a world of substitutions; it is one of the primitive substitutions that have guided the ancient history of human beings—this substitution is the history of the first death.

The multiple contradictions of capitalism show how the force of life is taken into the system of objective equivalents that take its place for the sake of accounting and calculation. These objective equivalents are all rooted in a duplication of the real process of production of use values by the economic process of the production of exchange values. In short, instead of favoring the exchange of products and stimulating their production, value stops them both at the same time. Money is always lacking. Production is no longer the problem but selling is. Between the subjectivity of production and the subjectivity of consumption, the economy builds up a wall of quantifiable and calculable idealities. They lead an almost autonomous existence and no longer have any perceivable connection with life. The original concordance between the life of production and consumption—which is identified with the movement of life and with the activity in view of satisfying the needs of life—is broken. Money is not only lacking due to the fact of exploitation, where the value produced by the worker surpasses his wage so that the worker is never able to buy or to consume what is produced. In addition, a deeper reason gives birth to the crisis that economists and governments are trying to manage. Marx's genius is to have seen the simple reason for this and to have anticipated that it would lead us outside of the capitalist system—beyond the economic world itself—and into the dangerous world toward which we are falling.

This time has already begun. Death insidiously expands its empire, without anyone noticing it. Its central but hidden characteristic is that capitalism progressively gives way to the modern essence of technology. Technology finds a place little by little in capitalism until it invades capitalism completely and, in the end, technology will establish its dominion in place of capitalism. This is a strange and imperceptible development, since one single law covers both of these domains. Passing from the capitalist world to the world of technology, technology offers the opportunity to dramatically increase its power for destruction and death.

In order to produce the surplus value which is an integral part of it, capitalism eventually had to renounce extending the work day. It was then that technology—the systematic automation of the real process of production—allowed it to achieve its objective: the creation of surplus value. And that is the decisive event—it is the Archi-fact that engendered and continues to engender modernity. Due to the unlimited extension of instrumental devices that tend to coincide with the process of production and to define it, living labor is increasingly excluded from this process. This principle—the exclusion of subjectivity—does not stem from capitalism but from Galilean science, and technology reveals its true sense.

Let's recall one last time that modern science—which was invented by Galileo and sought to provide a rational knowledge of the world—abstracts from the sensible qualities of the world. Its world is made up of extended material bodies whose figures and forms can only be grasped adequately by geometry. Descartes provides a mathematical formulation of this. To exclude the sensible qualities from the world is to exclude sensibility from it and, along with it, everything else that is subjective. It is thus to exclude life itself.

History is subsequently unified by capitalism and technology, or, what we have called the "technical-economic" world. It results from the projection of Galilean presuppositions onto human action. Human action is then overturned and undergoes an almost unfathomable ontological and metaphysical transubstantiation. Its nature changes. It no longer takes place in the subjectivity of human beings but in things. Living labor gives way to objective material processes that function on their own, regulate themselves, program themselves, and set the time of their own destruction. Along with the nature of action, its way of being known is totally changed. Unlike living labor, it is no longer the case that life knows itself through the experience of its own pathos. Instead, it is a geometric-mathematic knowledge. Modern physics and the sciences linked to it are the ones that understand and moreover construct the instrumental devices of technology.

When technology invades the real process of production to the point of becoming identical with it, there are two results that follow: living labor is eliminated from this process and, along with it, so too is the power of creating value and thus value itself. When the technical-economic universe has reached its goal and the process of production has become purely technological, there will no longer be any workers in the process of production and there will be no way for them to acquire its products, either. In Brazil, half of the population is already situated outside of the economic circuit: without work and without money. *All that is left is to produce objects that are no longer destined for human beings and to produce objects without them.*

–"Master, I'm afraid, I met death: it looked me in the eyes ..."

The most beautiful name is that of life. It is the most beautiful name because it refers to the mysterious and magical power that carries us like deep water; it is an ever-present power. It supports us; it never leaves or deceives us. It is constantly there, like a mother who would never separate herself from the child to whom she gave birth. It still gives birth and continues to give existence to the self. Life is there in its own way, in emotion, feeling, sensibility, suffering, and joy. It is the ineffable happiness of feeling oneself and of living. This happiness is so great and life is so desirable that, as Meister Eckhart says, one seeks to live even if one does not know why one is alive.

It is strange that modern thought remains silent on the subject of life. At least this is the case, if by life one does not mean the biological life that is composed of molecules and cells and that gains its title from the Galilean, scientific nobility, its laboratories, its funding, and its numerous researchers and advocates, and if by life one means what has been in question in these pages. This is the life of everyone and the life that everyone speaks about, the life of workers especially but also of idlers. Yet, it is even more strange that, if one happens to evoke this essence of our existence, it gives rise to a general anxiety and suspicions are raised. For there is a well-known doctrine about life, which is known for being confused as well as dangerous. This doctrine is called "vitalism," and it is true that it is located at the origin of the greatest literary and artistic creations of the end of the nineteenth century and the first half of the twentieth century. But, it is also the case that it is located at the origin of Nazism—where the blind exaltation of force led to the worst excesses and the greatest crimes.

The cause of these excesses and crimes as well as the confused thoughts that are placed under the heading of vitalism is the obscurity of the phenomena with which it is concerned and, first of all, with their common principle—life. This intrinsic obscurity of the vital force explains the "blindness" of the behaviors that are evoked by desires and drives, as along as the light of reason does not illuminate them in order to correct their trajectory or to cool their passion. The light of reason is equally the light of the world by which we see every thing, and the "light of the State" is a ray projected onto human affairs. It alone can save them from disorder and confrontation.

But, what if the "obscurity" of life is only a result of this self-proclaimed rationalism? What if it is only the result of its own blindness with respect to life, namely, its inability to recognize any other mode of revelation than the thought that sees and knows things and only sees them in this way—which only knows objects? The rejection of life, together with the rejection of the living individual, leads it into a subaltern condition where it is unable to direct itself, and where, precisely due to knowledge, it does not know what it should do. This results from a very long-standing prejudice according to which the only knowledge is objective knowledge. To know life is then to cast it outside of itself, into the "outside," into a horizon of light where things become visible, and into the world. This gives rise to the various processes of substitution that we have pursued in this work such as social classes, the economy, and politics. Naïve thought imagines that these domains exist on their own, for all times, although they are merely the products of processes of substitution. To know life means to keep account of it and to be able to calculate it so that it can be included in the broad field of objective and scientific knowledge. Due to this knowledge, it is at last torn away from its intrinsic obscurity. *It is not life but rationalism that is responsible for "vitalism," for this monstrous reduction of life to a blind and menacing power.*

Against the exorbitant attempts of objective thought and its supposed rationalism, life puts forward three counter-propositions. These are three ways by which it can hold its own fate in its hands and save itself—and the universe at the same time.

Instead of asking objective thought to make it manifest, life carries out the work of its own Revelation. This occurs through the experience of itself in the invincible certitude of its need, its effort, its suffering or its joy. It alone escapes from doubt. According to Descartes's general and decisive insight, even if the world did not exist and were only a dream, it would nonetheless remain as it is experienced.

Instead of being ex-posed in the light of this world and instead of being offered to the grasp of objective knowledge, life cannot ever do this. For, life is only ever present to itself in itself, in the undivided interiority of its own pathos. That is the reason why substitution—whatever precise form it might have in any given case—is only a representation of life. It is only a sign, an index, or an image; it is only something that stands for life but is not it. According to Marx's great and decisive insight, the economists' notion of abstract labor is real labor set in opposition to itself, placed in front of itself, and objectified. But, this is no longer real labor—it is only an abstraction instead of and in place of life. When thought thinks life, it performs an essential de-realization of life. When this is forgotten, the objective equivalents themselves claim to constitute reality, especially the reality of living subjectivity, and they simply take its place. Here a murder is carried out.

Instead of asking reason what it should do, life itself knows what it should do—and it alone knows this. It does not know what it should do through rational knowledge but in its own way—not through the discovery of an objective field of quantifiable and calculable phenomena but through the irrecusable experience of its desire and its passion. Life leads individuals to work in order to feed themselves; it leads couples to be formed and societies to exist. Life is the true Reason. It assigns specific goals to human beings. It has initially constructed these goals in them, and they reside in the irresistible movement of their drives and their love—in the movement of life.

Life is the only foundation of ethics. Ethics develops in the footsteps of life and follows its progress step by step. This happens through dramatic experiences that are nothing other than the various ways in which life comes into contact with its own Basis. Each time one of these experiences occurs—for instance, when a man allows his brother or enemy to go ahead of him or when he recognizes Life in the face of the Other—a law of ethics is affirmed by one of the "great affective geniuses of history" with an irresistible force. But they truly know nothing about its "objective conditions," nor do they conduct a situational analysis. For, the greatest force arises within such experiences and allows one to experience that one is alive. This experience resides even in the smallest of our gestures, the most routine acts, inasmuch as the greatest force resides in them too and makes them possible.

We can now at last take stock of a universe from which life has been excluded. Life has been replaced by society, the people, history, social classes, by economic entities like money, profit, interest and their respective rates, or by material reality in the case of modern technology—by definition, this is a universe of death. When the organizing principle of the world is something that feels nothing and does not feel itself—something that has no desire or love—this brings about a time of madness. For, this madness has lost everything except reason. How could one fail to notice the affinity established between the regimes that strive for an exhaustive and rational planning of society—they claim to be built on the basis of objective knowledge of all material and social phenomena and that their society is the synthesis of all of the phenomena that they can imagine—and modern technology, which is a complex of material processes torn from nature and regulated by the very same geometrical-mathematical knowledge from which all subjectivity is removed? Communism is a radical rationalism. It is not the first systematic attempt to think rationally but the first to regulate human activity as if it were a system of objective relations—like a pure object—that is foreign to life. Communism is not opposed to the Western, American, or Japanese world of technology: it is a precursor to it, its first aborted attempt. Is not the Plan itself a form of calculation that is put under the control of the universe? When Lenin said that communism is electricity and the Soviets, he was indeed the precursor of Brezhnev who expected salvation by computers. The journal of the French communist party is called "La Pensée" (*Thought*). This is only an apparent paradox, because it is in fact the most honorable title for materialism.

But one cannot get rid of life so easily—it never gets rid of oneself and adheres to the self with all of its invincible force. One can try to replace life by projecting new worlds beyond life. The most terrible one of them is the one that turns the exclusion of subjectivity into the law of its development. Life continues to exist nonetheless, leaning on itself and not renouncing itself. Life is stripped of all the goods it has acquired over the course of centuries and of all the works that it has constructed in order to experience the joy of life more intensely—to ensure the simple possibility of continuing to live. Life is left without culture, without art, without memory, without religion. Life is reduced artificially to the abstractions that claim to replace it and ends up being reduced to material processes that are homogenous with the objective world and derived from the same type of knowledge as it. Life's infinite Desire, limitless imagination, and love become "natural needs." They become knowable and explicable as material processes as well. They are known through science and through reason—they are calculated, predicted, and planned.

Nonetheless, life continues to live in spite of being flouted, humiliated, theoretically devalued, and set aside. Capitalism retains it as the sole creative force of value and also, at the other end of the process, as the subjectivity of consumption. Capitalism has not yet learned how to do without it entirely. Capitalism addresses this life that has been deprived of everything that could have increased and exalted it. It tries to sell everything that it can still sell to its lowest needs—it sells objects at a reduced price, manufactured by a miserable workforce chosen for its misery, all kinds of junk, music for mental imbeciles, products reduced to advertised images, air bubbles, and cardboard beaches. One wants to get what one deserves.

The empty subjectivity of the West is a voracious subjectivity: it does not stay in place. Like the fish that it has observed, it launches itself toward everything that moves, toward the crumbs that are thrown to it, toward all the lures. For it has been taught to desire lures, and lures are the only things that can satisfy it—provided that there are other ones. The European ministers of Culture assure us that the flow of television images will continue to increase.

Under the reign of technology, capitalism must sell especially those things that have no relation to life and that do not matter to life in any way. It must sell so-called "communication" satellites, although in this particular form of communication no one communicates with anyone else. It sells spaceships, inter-continental and inter-planetary rockets, advanced engines, and surreal telescopes. It sells supercomputers whose material operations are said to be identical to the operations of thought, such that thought must now learn to function like them, without feeling anything, without wanting anything—without thinking! The resemblance of these lures with the inert makes them fascinating. This is the future of entropy and of the universe itself, the avowed goal of life, *if it is defined as a death drive*. We know the true name of this self-negation of life; we now know its sinister face and nauseating odor; we know the regimes for which it is the principle.

Those who seek to escape from death by going to the West do not yet know that death awaits them at a rendezvous. Regardless of being devalued, oppressed, exhausted, and overtaken, the force that lifts up individuals is the force of life. The lures in cardboard—the fries at McDonald's—will only deceive them once. The truth that shines in their eyes is neither the truth of democracy nor of capitalism—nor is it the truth of technology or science fiction. It is the truth, which has long been hidden, that was proclaimed in the night of Prague. The truth is a cry: it is the cry of life, which says that it is life and that it wants to live.

NOTES

Translator's Preface

1   Michel Henry, *Marx: A Philosophy of Human Reality*, trans. Kathleen McLaughlin (Bloomington: Indiana University Press, 1983). Michel Henry, *Barbarism*, trans. Scott Davidson (London: Continuum, 2012).

Introduction

1   See his "Les atouts de Gorbatchev: une évaluation" in *Après Gorbatchev* (Paris: La Table Ronde, 1990).

Chapter One

1   The third of these—the *1844 Manuscripts*—does not have the same sense. Under the direct influence of Feuerbach, it is still dependent on the Hegelianism against which Marx will come to define his own original thought.

2   Translator's note: this is a reference to the character Rosalie who states at the end of Maupassant's book: "You see, life's neither as good nor as bad as we think." Guy De Maupassant, *A Life: The Humble Truth*, trans. Roger Pearson (Oxford: Oxford University Press, 1999).

3   Meister Eckhart, *The Essential Sermons, Commentaries, Treatises, and Defenses* (Mahwah, NJ: Paulist Press, 1981), 186–7.

4   Karl Marx, "Theses on Feuerbach," First Thesis.

5   These expressions are repeatedly introduced, especially in the *Grundrisse* and *Capital*.

6   In his critique of monarchy, Marx denies Hegel the right to include sovereignty in one individual to the detriment of all the others, and continually insists on the infinite plurality of living individuals. See his "Critique of Hegel's Philosophy of the State," where Marx states that "the ideality of the state as person, as subject, exists evidently as many persons, many subjects."

7   Karl Marx, *The German Ideology* (Amherst, NY: Prometheus Books, 1976), "The first premise of all human history is, of course, the existence of living human individuals" (107). And later, "the premises from which we begin are real individuals" (112).

8   See Marx, *The German Ideology*.

9   Max Stirner, *The Ego and its Own,* trans. David Leopold (Cambridge: Cambridge University Press, 1995).

10   It is in this simplified and completely erroneous way that Engels presents Marx's thought, after his death, in his work *Ludwig Feuerbach and the End of Classical German Philosophy* (Moscow: Progress Publishers, 1886). This fallacious work and the conceptual poverty of this motto provided the theoretical foundation for Marxism, while the fundamental philosophical writings of Marx remained unknown.

Chapter Two

1   Marx, *The German Ideology*, 271.

2   Karl Marx, *The Poverty of Philosophy* (New York: International Publishers), 91.

3   Marx, *The German Ideology*, 511.

4   Marx, "Theses on Feuerbach," First Thesis.

Chapter Three

1   Translator's note: I have retained the French *ressentiment* in order to highlight a potential connection to Nietzsche's use of the term. It appears henceforth in the text in italics.

2   Marx, *The German Ideology*, 85 (Marx's italics).

3   Marx, *The German Ideology*, 85 (Henry's italics).

4   Marx, *The German Ideology*, 380.

5   Marx, *The German Ideology,* 380 (Henry's italics).

6   Marx, *The German Ideology*, ch. 3.

Chapter Four

1   Marx, "Critique of the Gotha Program," in Karl Marx and Frederick Engels, *Selected Works* (London: Lawrence and Wishart, 1968), 324.

Chapter Five

1   Marx, *Grundrisse: Foundations of the Critique of Political Economy,* trans. Martin Nicolaus (New York: Vintage Books, 1973), 312.

2   Marx, *The German Ideology,* 46.

Chapter Six

1   Karl Marx, "Critique of the Gotha Program," 324.

Chapter Seven

1   Galileo, "The Assayer," in *Selected Writings*, trans. William R Shea and Mark Davie (Oxford: Oxford University Press, 2012).

Chapter Eight

1   Karl Marx, "Critique of Hegel's Philosophy of the State," in *Early Writings*, trans. Rodney Livingstone and Gregor Benton (New York: Vintage Books, 1975), 83.

Conclusion

1   The text is from a twelfth century Persian fable by Farid Al-Din Attar.

2   Translator's note: Henry says this in reference to the Katyn Massacre,
    which was a mass execution of Polish nationals under the orders of Stalin.

INDEX